BRITAIN BY ATLAS 2026

THE ULTIMATE GUIDE TO ICONIC ROUTES, HIDDEN GEMS & MUST-SEE DESTINATIONS BY RAIL

KASHTON TIKHON

Copyright © 2025 by KASHTON TIKHON
All Rights Reserved.

No portion of this publication may be reproduced, distributed, or transmitted in any form or by any means—electronic, mechanical, or otherwise—without prior written consent from the publisher, except for brief quotations used in reviews, academic works, or as permitted under U.S. copyright law and fair use.

This publication is protected under international copyright regulations. Unauthorized use, reproduction, or distribution is strictly prohibited and may result in legal consequences. For permission inquiries, please contact the publisher.

Disclaimer and Terms of Use

This book is intended for general informational and educational purposes. Although every effort has been made to ensure the accuracy and reliability of the information at the time of publication, neither the author nor the publisher guarantees its completeness or suitability for any particular purpose.

The material provided is not a substitute for professional legal, financial, medical, or other expert advice. Any actions you take based on the content of this book are done at your own discretion and risk. The author and publisher assume no responsibility for any outcomes—favorable or unfavorable—that result from the use or misinterpretation of the information contained herein.

By continuing to read this book, you acknowledge and accept full responsibility for your choices and actions.

Printed in the United States of America.

TABLE OF CONTENT

TABLE OF CONTENT III

CHAPTER 1 INTRODUCTION TO BRITAIN'S RAIL ADVENTURES 1
- *The Allure of Train Travel in Britain* 2
- *Key Train Routes to Know* 3
- *Rail Passes & Tickets: Maximizing Your Experience* 6

OVERVIEW OF THE UK RAIL NETWORK 7
- *Key Train Operators and Services* 9
- *Ticketing, Passes, and Practical Travel Tips* 10

HOW TO PLAN YOUR SCENIC JOURNEY 12
- *Choose Your Route Wisely* 13
- *Booking and Rail Passes* 14
- *Packing and Onboard Essentials* 15

ESSENTIAL TRAVEL TIPS FOR TRAIN EXPLORERS 18
- *Planning Your Train Journey* 18
- *Navigating Stations and Transfers* 20
- *Experiencing the Scenery* 21
- *Cultural Insights for Rail Travelers* 23

CHAPTER 2 SOUTHERN ENGLAND: CASTLES, COASTLINES & HISTORY 25
- *Key Train Routes in Southern England* 26
- *Hidden Gems in Southern England* 30

BATH TO BRIGHTON: A GEORGIAN & SEASIDE ADVENTURE 32
- *Getting There: Train Connections & Timing* 32
- *Suggested Day Trip or Short Break* 36

EXPLORING STONEHENGE FROM SALISBURY BY RAIL 37
- *Getting to Salisbury by Train* 37
- *Getting to Stonehenge from Salisbury* 39

HIDDEN VILLAGES AND SEASIDE ESCAPES ON THE SOUTH COAST 43
- *Planning Your South Coast Journey* 43
- *Hidden Villages Worth the Journey* 44
- *Scenic Coastal Routes by Train* 46
- *Walking and Exploration Tips* 50

CHAPTER 3 THE COTSWOLDS & OXFORD: IDYLLIC COUNTRYSIDE BY RAIL 52
- *Highlights of the Cotswolds by Rail* 53
- *Getting to Oxford by Train* 55

SCENIC JOURNEYS THROUGH PICTURESQUE VILLAGES 57
- *Cotswolds Villages: Honey-Coloured Stone & Market Towns* 59
- *Scottish Highlands: Villages with Dramatic Backdrops* 60

OXFORD: THE CITY OF DREAMING SPIRES 63

Oxford Station to the City Center 64
Walking the City and Punting on the Rivers 65
Practical Map for Rail Travelers 67
A SLOW TRAVEL DAY IN THE HEART OF THE COTSWOLDS 68
Getting There by Train 69
Afternoon: Village Hopping by Train and Foot 70

CHAPTER 4 NORTHERN ENGLAND: PEAKS, PUBS & LAKES 73

Getting to Northern England by Train 74
The Peak District: Majestic Hills and Quaint Villages 76
THE LAKE DISTRICT: HIKING & LAKESIDE VIEWS FROM THE TRAIN 78
Key Train Routes to the Lake District 79
Coniston & Hawkshead: Northern Lakeside Adventures 82
THE YORKSHIRE DALES: EXPLORING NATURE AND HERITAGE 84
Getting to the Yorkshire Dales by Train 85
Exploring Natural Landscapes 86
MANCHESTER TO NEWCASTLE: URBAN MEETS COUNTRYSIDE 89
Planning the Journey 89
Mid-Morning: Heading Into Countryside 91
Arrival in Newcastle 93

CHAPTER 5 SCOTLAND'S HIGHLANDS & WILDERNESS BY RAIL 95

Getting to Scotland's Highlands by Train 95
Highlights of the Scottish Highlands by Rail 96
The Isle of Skye: Scotland's Rugged Beauty 98
THE WEST HIGHLAND LINE: SCOTLAND'S MOST SCENIC JOURNEY 100
Key Train Routes and Stations 100
EDINBURGH TO INVERNESS: A RIDE THROUGH HISTORY AND NATURE 104
Getting Started: Edinburgh Waverley Station 105
Key Stops and Experiences Along the Way 106
SKYE & LOCH NESS: MAJESTIC LANDSCAPES AND LEGENDS 110
Planning Your Highland Journey 110

CHAPTER 6 WALES: MOUNTAINS, COASTLINES & CASTLES BY TRAIN 116

Highlights of Wales by Rail 117
The Pembrokeshire Coast: Wild Beaches and Scenic Villages 119
CONWY TO SNOWDONIA: A JOURNEY THROUGH WELSH HISTORY 121
Key Train Routes and Connections 122
Llandudno Junction and Coastal Charm 123
Blaenau Ffestiniog: Slate History and Mountain Access 125
THE BRECON BEACONS: EXPLORE BY TRAIN AND FOOT 127
Getting to the Brecon Beacons by Train 127
Walking and Outdoor Adventures 130

    Cardiff to Pembrokeshire: A Coastal Escape 132

CHAPTER 7 138

THE GREAT WESTERN ROUTE: BRISTOL TO CORNWALL 138

    Getting Started: The Departure from Bristol 138

  BRISTOL: THE CULTURAL GATEWAY TO THE WEST 142

    Getting to Bristol by Train 142

    Historic City Center and Cultural Highlights 143

  DISCOVERING CORNWALL'S COASTLINE AND HIDDEN CORNERS 146

    Getting to Cornwall by Train 147

    Exploring Coastal Scenery 148

  WALKING AND OUTDOOR ACTIVITIES 149

  EXPLORING THE COASTAL RAILWAY BETWEEN DEVON AND CORNWALL 151

    Late Morning: Newton Abbot to Torbay 153

CHAPTER 8 PRACTICAL TRAVEL TIPS FOR 2026 TRAIN EXPLORERS 157

    Choosing the Right Ticket and Pass 157

    Navigating Train Stations: Arrival and Transfers 158

    Hidden Gems by Rail: Regional Highlights to Explore 160

  BOOKING TICKETS & RAIL PASSES FOR BEST VALUE 160

    Understanding the UK Rail Network 161

    Rail Passes for Multi-Region Travel 162

  NAVIGATING TRAIN STATIONS & TRANSFERS 165

    Understanding British Train Stations 165

    Planning Transfers Between Trains 166

  SEASONAL INSIGHTS: BEST TIME TO TRAVEL FOR SCENIC JOURNEYS 169

    Spring: Fresh Landscapes and Blooming Views 169

    Summer: Long Days and Vibrant Coastlines 170

    Autumn: Golden Hues and Quiet Villages 171

    Winter: Snow, Storms, and Atmospheric Landscapes 172

    Practical Travel Advice for Seasonal Planning 173

CHAPTER 1
INTRODUCTION TO BRITAIN'S RAIL ADVENTURES

Britain is a country brimming with rich history, scenic landscapes, and charming villages, all easily accessible by its extensive rail network. Whether you're seeking iconic landmarks, hidden gems, or breathtaking vistas, exploring Britain by train is one of the best ways to experience its diverse regions. From the bustling cities of London and Edinburgh to the quiet beauty of the Lake District and Scottish Highlands, trains offer a comfortable, efficient, and sustainable way to explore the heart of the UK.

Iconic & Scenic Train Journeys in the UK

This travel guide will take you on a journey across the most scenic and iconic train routes in Britain. It will highlight must-see destinations, offer tips on how to make the most of your rail adventure, and provide insights into the local culture, food, and seasonal best times to travel. Along the way, you'll discover the very essence of what makes Britain by rail an unforgettable experience.

Train travel in Britain regional atlas

THE ALLURE OF TRAIN TRAVEL IN BRITAIN

Train travel in Britain is more than just a means of getting from one place to another. It's an experience in itself. The country's rail network is one of the oldest in the world, with trains weaving through picturesque landscapes, winding around coastal cliffs, passing through dense forests, and cutting across vast moors. For those who prefer to sit back and take in the views, Britain's trains offer a perfect vantage point.

But it's not just about the scenery—train travel in Britain is steeped in history, with many routes linked to iconic events and locations. From the Great Western Railway, which once connected London to the West Country, to the East Coast Main Line, which offers spectacular views of the North Sea, each route has its own unique story to tell.

Why Choose Rail Travel?

There are several reasons why train travel is the preferred option for many visitors to Britain:

- **Accessibility**: Britain's rail network is comprehensive, covering almost every corner of the country. Even remote villages are often reachable by train, making it easy to explore off-the-beaten-path destinations.

- **Scenic Routes**: Few countries can offer such a variety of stunning landscapes seen from the comfort of a train window. From the rugged beauty of the Scottish Highlands to the peaceful countryside of the Cotswolds, train journeys in Britain are a scenic experience in themselves.

- **Sustainability**: Trains are a more sustainable mode of transport compared to cars or flights. With growing concerns over environmental impact, traveling by rail allows you to explore Britain while reducing your carbon footprint.

- **Convenience**: Britain's trains are known for their punctuality and frequency, making it a hassle-free way to travel between destinations. Many routes are also connected to local bus services, offering seamless onward travel to more remote spots.

KEY TRAIN ROUTES TO KNOW

While there are countless scenic routes across Britain, here are some of the must-try journeys that will take you through the heart of the country's natural beauty and historic landmarks:

West Highland Line (Scotland)

One of the most famous rail journeys in the world, the West Highland Line travels from Glasgow to Mallaig, offering awe-inspiring views of lochs, mountains, and coastline. This route takes you deep into the Scottish Highlands, where the natural beauty is nothing short of breathtaking.

- **Highlights**: Loch Lomond, Ben Nevis, and the viaduct made famous by the Harry Potter films.

- **When to Go**: The journey is stunning year-round, but the best time to travel is late spring or early autumn when the landscape is especially vibrant.

West Highland Line (Scotland) train route

The Settle-Carlisle Line (England)

For a truly authentic British rail experience, the Settle-Carlisle Line is a must. Running through the Yorkshire Dales and into the heart of the Cumbrian Fells, this historic line passes over 72 bridges, including the famous Ribblehead Viaduct.

- **Highlights**: The grandeur of the Ribblehead Viaduct, the beautiful Cumbrian countryside, and the rolling hills of the Yorkshire Dales.
- **When to Go**: Summer is ideal, but autumn brings out the dramatic beauty of the landscape, with the changing colors of the foliage.

The East Coast Main Line (England and Scotland)

This high-speed route runs from London to Edinburgh, offering views of the North Sea, picturesque coastal towns, and some of the UK's most iconic landmarks, including Durham Cathedral and the ancient city of York.

- **Highlights**: The views of the North Sea, the historic cities of Durham, York, and Edinburgh, and the vast, open landscapes of Northumberland.

- **When to Go**: Autumn and winter are the most dramatic, but spring and summer bring pleasant weather for longer journeys.

The Great Western Railway (England)

This historic route, once described as the "King of the Railways," links London to the southwest of England, passing through the stunning countryside of Devon and Cornwall. It offers one of the most beautiful coastal routes in the UK.

The Great Western Railway (England) regions

- **Highlights**: The coastlines of Cornwall, the rolling hills of Devon, and the historic cities of Bath and Bristol.
- **When to Go**: Spring and summer, when the countryside is at its greenest and coastal areas enjoy pleasant weather.

The Jacobite Steam Train (Scotland)

If you're looking for an iconic experience, then nothing beats riding the Jacobite Steam Train, which operates on the West Highland Line. Famously used as the Hogwarts Express in the Harry Potter films, this nostalgic journey offers a unique way to travel through some of Scotland's most remote and breathtaking landscapes.

- **Highlights**: Glenfinnan Viaduct, the stunning backdrop of the Scottish Highlands, and the charm of the steam train experience.
- **When to Go**: The Jacobite operates seasonally, from April to October, with the best views in early summer.

RAIL PASSES & TICKETS: MAXIMIZING YOUR EXPERIENCE

If you're planning to travel extensively by train in Britain, a rail pass can offer great value for money. The **BritRail Pass** is available for tourists, allowing unlimited travel on the British rail network for a set number of days. For those who prefer more flexibility, **Advance Tickets** can be purchased online, often at discounted rates if booked in advance.

Using Your Rail Pass

For shorter journeys, single tickets are easy to purchase from station ticket machines or online, but be mindful that prices can vary based on time and availability. The earlier you book, the better the prices.

Essential Travel Tips

- **Plan Your Routes**: While Britain's rail network is extensive, it's still a good idea to plan your journey in advance. This will help you ensure you're on the best trains for the most scenic routes and avoid long waits at stations.

- **Pack Smart**: Many trains in Britain offer ample space for luggage, but it's always best to pack light for ease of movement. A comfortable backpack or small suitcase should suffice for most trips.
- **Consider Local Transfers**: While most major towns and cities are well connected by rail, some remote areas may require a local bus or taxi for the last leg of the journey. Check ahead to make sure your destination is accessible by public transport.
- **Seasonal Travel**: While trains run year-round, some routes, especially in rural and coastal areas, are busier in the summer months. If you prefer less crowded trains, opt for spring or autumn travel when the weather is still favorable, but the crowds have thinned out.
- **Food and Drink on Board**: Many long-distance trains, especially on the West Coast Main Line and Great Western Railway, offer dining options ranging from light snacks to full meals. For shorter journeys, consider picking up a picnic at the station to enjoy while taking in the views.
- **Mind the Weather**: British weather can be unpredictable, so it's wise to pack layers and be prepared for rain, especially if you're traveling in winter or autumn. Having a good pair of waterproof shoes is always a smart choice.

Exploring Britain by train offers an enriching travel experience, combining convenience, comfort, and scenic beauty all in one. Whether you're traversing the rolling hills of the Cotswolds, gazing out over the rugged Scottish Highlands, or soaking up the charm of historic cities like Bath and York, the train journey will become as memorable as the destination itself.

By carefully selecting your routes, timing your trips to match the seasons, and embracing the unique experiences that each destination has to offer, you'll make the most of your time in Britain. So, pack your bags, grab your rail pass, and embark on an unforgettable adventure across the UK's landscapes.

OVERVIEW OF THE UK RAIL NETWORK

Traveling by train across Britain offers an unmatched perspective on the country's history, culture, and landscapes. The UK rail network is one of the densest and most comprehensive in Europe, connecting major cities, charming towns, and remote rural areas with ease. Whether you are a first-time visitor or a seasoned rail traveler, understanding the structure, key routes, ticketing, and practical tips will enhance every journey.

UK rail network atlas

The Structure of the Network

The UK rail network is divided into multiple regions and services, operated by different train companies under the umbrella of National Rail. The main network spans **over 16,000 kilometers**, connecting England, Scotland, and Wales. Northern Ireland has a separate system, primarily run by NI Railways, with fewer but scenic connections.

The network is structured around several hubs:

- **London**: The capital is the main gateway to the country, with major terminals like **King's Cross**, **Euston**, **Paddington**, **Liverpool Street**, and **Waterloo** serving different regions. Each station acts as a departure point for intercity, regional, and local services.

- **Northern England & Midlands**: Key cities such as Manchester, Leeds, Sheffield, Birmingham, and Nottingham are linked via high-speed and regional services.
- **Scotland**: Edinburgh, Glasgow, and Aberdeen are primary hubs, with scenic connections through the Highlands and to the Western Isles.
- **Wales**: Cardiff, Swansea, and Holyhead provide both regional services and access to coastal and rural destinations.

Trains range from **high-speed intercity services** (e.g., LNER and Avanti West Coast) to slower **regional and local services**, which often serve smaller villages and scenic routes.

KEY TRAIN OPERATORS AND SERVICES

Understanding the main train operators helps plan journeys efficiently:

- **LNER (London North Eastern Railway)**: Fast trains connecting London King's Cross with York, Newcastle, and Edinburgh. Offers spectacular routes along the East Coast Main Line, ideal for countryside and coastal scenery.
- **Avanti West Coast**: High-speed service linking London Euston with Birmingham, Manchester, Liverpool, and Glasgow. The route passes through the dramatic landscapes of the Lake District and the Scottish Lowlands.
- **Great Western Railway (GWR)**: Serves London Paddington to the West Country, South Wales, and the Cotswolds. Trains provide scenic coastal views near Cornwall and Devon.
- **ScotRail**: Regional services across Scotland, including the famous West Highland Line and Caledonian Sleeper services to London.
- **Northern Trains & TransPennine Express**: Cover Northern England, connecting industrial cities with the Pennines, Yorkshire Dales, and Lake District.
- **Transport for Wales (TfW Rail)**: Provides comprehensive coverage of Wales, including access to Snowdonia, Pembrokeshire, and coastal towns.

Each operator has its own ticketing and seating options. Most major routes allow **advance booking**, which is cheaper, while **off-peak returns** and **rail passes** (like the BritRail Pass) offer flexibility for tourists.

Interpreting the Network Map

When planning train travel, understanding the geography and connectivity is crucial. Major lines radiate from London like spokes on a wheel:

- **East Coast Main Line**: London → Cambridge → York → Newcastle → Edinburgh
- **West Coast Main Line**: London → Birmingham → Manchester → Liverpool → Glasgow
- **Great Western Main Line**: London → Reading → Bath → Bristol → South Wales → South West England
- **Cross-Country Routes**: Birmingham ↔ Bristol ↔ Cardiff ↔ Edinburgh, connecting mid-sized cities across regions without returning to London

Regional lines often branch off these main arteries, reaching smaller towns and scenic destinations. For example, from Carlisle, the **Settle–Carlisle Line** winds through the Yorkshire Dales with some of the most dramatic railway landscapes in the UK.

Practical Tip: Many scenic lines are single-track and lightly serviced. Check schedules in advance, especially in rural areas, where trains may run only a few times per day.

TICKETING, PASSES, AND PRACTICAL TRAVEL TIPS

Traveling the UK by train is made simpler with the right knowledge:

- **National Rail Tickets**: Standard, Off-Peak, and Advance fares are widely available. Booking early is often cheaper.

National Rail ticket

- **BritRail Passes**: Ideal for non-UK residents planning multiple journeys; they allow unlimited travel across most routes.
- **Railcards**: Discounted travel for seniors, youths, and families. For example, a 16–25 Railcard offers 1/3 off fares.
- **Seat Reservations**: Recommended for long intercity journeys. Some regional trains don't require reservations, making them flexible for spontaneous travel.
- **Apps and Online Tools**: National Rail Enquiries, Trainline, and operator-specific apps are essential for checking real-time schedules and disruptions.

Seasonal Considerations

Rail travel in Britain can vary dramatically by season:

- **Spring (March–May)**: Ideal for scenic routes; rolling hills and gardens bloom across the countryside. Lines such as the **Cotswold Line** and **North Yorkshire Moors Railway** offer picturesque landscapes.
- **Summer (June–August)**: Long daylight hours and festival season make this peak tourist time. Trains to coastal towns like St Ives, Brighton, or Cornwall are busy; early bookings are recommended.
- **Autumn (September–November)**: The network is less crowded, and foliage adds vibrant color to routes such as the **West Highland Line** and the **Cambrian Coast Line**.
- **Winter (December–February)**: Railways remain reliable, though services to remote areas may be limited during snow. Cities like Edinburgh and Bath are beautiful for holiday markets.

Practical Insight from Experience

Having traveled across Britain extensively by train, I've learned that **small stations often hold hidden treasures**. For example:

- **Berwick-upon-Tweed** (East Coast Main Line) is a charming border town with historic walls, accessible by a short walk from the station.
- **Oxenhope** (near Keighley, West Yorkshire) on the heritage **Keighley & Worth Valley Railway** is ideal for steam train enthusiasts.

- **Portree** (Isle of Skye) requires a bus from Kyle of Lochalsh station, but the journey along the **Kyle Line** offers unmatched Highland scenery.

Transfers are generally smooth, as most stations provide local bus and taxi connections. Many smaller towns are pedestrian-friendly, so you can explore without renting a car.

Food Tip: Many stations now have artisan cafes, but for authentic local cuisine, venture a short walk into town. Try Cornish pasties in Penzance, haggis in Inverness, or Welsh cakes in Conwy.

Advantages of Traveling by Train in Britain

- **Scenic Access**: Some of the most breathtaking landscapes, like the Lake District, Scottish Highlands, and Cornish coast, are best appreciated from rail.
- **Environmental Benefits**: Trains are a greener alternative to cars or domestic flights.
- **Convenience**: Central station locations allow easy access to city centers without the hassle of parking.
- **Flexibility**: Day trips and multi-stop journeys are feasible thanks to frequent services and regional connections.

Mastering the UK rail network is the first step to exploring Britain's diverse landscapes, historic cities, and hidden gems. From high-speed intercity connections to serene rural lines, traveling by train offers unmatched comfort, convenience, and scenic enjoyment. Knowing the key routes, operators, seasonal variations, and practical tips ensures that every journey is not only smooth but also memorable.

The next chapters of this atlas will guide you along **specific scenic routes, seasonal highlights, and hidden treasures**, giving step-by-step instructions on how to turn a simple rail journey into an unforgettable adventure.

HOW TO PLAN YOUR SCENIC JOURNEY

Traveling through Britain by train offers a rare combination of convenience, history, and natural beauty. From sweeping coastlines to misty highlands, Britain's rail network connects bustling cities with charming villages, making it perfect for a scenic journey. Planning your trip well ensures you see iconic sights, hidden gems, and experience local culture fully. This guide will help you plan a seamless journey that balances comfort, exploration, and adventure.

Best Scenic Train Rides in Europe | Interrail

CHOOSE YOUR ROUTE WISELY

Britain has a dense rail network, but not all lines offer equal scenic value. Focus on routes that showcase diverse landscapes and cultural highlights. Popular scenic routes include:

- **The West Highland Line (Glasgow to Mallaig, Scotland)**: Famous for mountains, lochs, and the Glenfinnan Viaduct (the "Harry Potter bridge").

- **Settle-Carlisle Railway (Yorkshire to Cumbria, England)**: Rolling hills, viaducts, and remote villages.

- **Cambrian Line (Shrewsbury to Aberystwyth, Wales)**: Coastal cliffs, beaches, and scenic countryside.

- **Cornish Main Line (Penzance to Plymouth, England)**: Seaside views, quaint fishing towns, and historical harbors.

Pro tip: Decide whether your journey is destination-focused or experience-focused. If your goal is landscapes, prioritize coastal and mountain lines. For cultural immersion, choose routes passing through historical towns or markets.

Timing and Seasons

Scenic rail journeys change dramatically with the seasons.

- **Spring (March–May)**: Blooming gardens, milder weather, and fewer crowds. Ideal for routes like the Cotswolds or Scottish Borders.

- **Summer (June–August)**: Long daylight hours and vibrant scenery. Coastal lines, like the Cornish Main Line, are particularly spectacular. However, trains may be crowded. Advance booking is essential.

- **Autumn (September–November)**: Golden landscapes, especially in Yorkshire, Lake District, and the Highlands. Cooler weather makes hiking feasible around stations.

- **Winter (December–February)**: Low tourist density, atmospheric scenery, and festive markets. Certain remote lines, like the West Highland Line, may run limited services—check timetables.

Travel insight: If photography or videography is a priority, plan your train ride to align with sunrise or sunset. West-facing coastal routes offer breathtaking light in late afternoon.

BOOKING AND RAIL PASSES

Britain's rail system can be navigated with single tickets, but scenic travelers benefit from rail passes for flexibility:

- **BritRail Pass**: Ideal for international travelers. Covers most UK railways and allows unlimited travel on consecutive or flexible days.

- **Regional Passes**: Such as the **Scotland Explorer Pass** or **Heart of Wales Pass**, often cheaper for local journeys.

- **Advance Tickets**: Available on National Rail, often cheaper but less flexible. Use these for long-distance scenic routes like the Settle-Carlisle or West Highland Line.

Practical tip: Some small rural stations do not accept card payments. Carry a small amount of cash for tickets or station kiosks.

Train Types and Comfort

Understanding train types enhances your journey:

- **InterCity Express (ICE/Avanti, CrossCountry)**: Fast, comfortable, suitable for long distances. Reserved seating is recommended.
- **Scenic Regional Trains (ScotRail, Great Western Railway, Northern Rail)**: Slightly slower but panoramic windows and local charm.
- **Steam or Heritage Lines (e.g., Ffestiniog Railway, North Yorkshire Moors Railway)**: Perfect for nostalgia and photography; less practical for strict schedules.

Travel insight: For long journeys, book window seats on the left or right depending on direction—local guides often note which side offers the best views.

Planning Connections and Transfers

Britain's scenic stations are often small and remote. Connections matter:

- **Glasgow to Mallaig**: Direct, but in summer, book early to secure a window seat. Mallaig offers ferry connections to Skye.
- **Settle-Carlisle**: Single-train service most of the year. Station stops are brief; prepare in advance if you want to disembark for photos.
- **Cornish Line**: Trains are frequent; Penzance and St Ives are linked by bus if you want extra coastal stops.
- **Heart of Wales Line**: Limited frequency. Check timetable carefully to avoid long waits.

Walking tip: Many rural stations are surrounded by trails and viewpoints. Research walking routes in advance, especially near scenic viaducts or cliffs.

PACKING AND ONBOARD ESSENTIALS

A scenic train journey may involve variable weather, especially in coastal or highland areas. Pack smart:

- **Light layers** for fluctuating temperatures.
- **Waterproof jacket and sturdy shoes** for short hikes near stations.
- **Travel snacks and refillable water**; some rural trains have limited catering.
- **Camera or smartphone** for panoramic shots.

Optional but useful: binoculars for spotting wildlife or distant landscapes, especially in Scottish and Welsh highlands.

Local Experiences and Stopovers

Scenic train travel is not just about the ride—it's about the stops:

- **Scottish Highlands**: Stop at Fort William for hiking Ben Nevis or visiting Glen Nevis. The Jacobite Steam Train offers a nostalgic detour to Mallaig.
- **Yorkshire Dales**: Settle station is ideal for walks to Ribblehead Viaduct and local pubs serving hearty local fare.
- **Cornwall**: Alight at St Ives for art galleries, coastal walks, and Cornish pasties. Penzance has historic harbors and nearby Minack Theatre.
- **Wales**: Aberystwyth's coastline offers sandy beaches and castle ruins. Local buses connect nearby trails.

Cultural insight: Many smaller stations host weekend markets or festivals. Align your stops with local events for an authentic experience.

Food and Dining Options

Rail travel can be an opportunity to taste regional cuisine:

- **Station Cafés and Pubs**: Many rural stations have nearby inns offering locally sourced dishes. For example, Settle's Sun Inn serves classic Yorkshire pies.
- **Onboard Catering**: Long-distance trains often provide hot meals and snacks. For a truly scenic experience, pack a picnic from a local market.
- **Specialty Stops**: Cornwall for cream teas, Scottish Highlands for smoked salmon or locally brewed ales, Wales for lamb dishes.

Insider tip: Train stations with local food markets, such as St Albans or Whitby, allow you to pick up artisanal snacks for the journey.

Digital and Paper Tools for Navigation

Planning a scenic journey requires accurate information:

- **Rail Timetable Apps**: National Rail Enquiries, Trainline, or ScotRail apps provide real-time schedules.

- **Offline Maps**: Some remote lines have limited signal; download maps beforehand.
- **Guidebooks and Local Leaflets**: Often available at stations; provide hidden trails and viewpoints not widely known.

Pro tip: Take a small notebook or phone app to log viewpoints, stops, or dining recommendations for future trips.

Safety and Accessibility

Safety is straightforward but worth considering:

- **Train Safety**: Hold handrails when moving; most scenic trains traverse viaducts or steep areas.
- **Weather Preparedness**: Fog or rain can affect visibility in highlands. Check weather forecasts before departure.
- **Accessibility**: Most mainline stations are accessible. For remote lines, check in advance if lifts or ramps are available.

Creating Your Personal Scenic Map

Finally, design your journey with a visual map:

- **Identify your start and end points**, including major scenic stops.
- **Mark local transfers**—buses, ferries, or walking trails.
- **Highlight overnight stays**, focusing on towns with local culture or easy access to train stations.
- **Include seasonal notes**—best times for light, wildlife, or festivals.

Example:

- **Glasgow → Fort William → Mallaig**: Overnight in Fort William. Ferry to Isle of Skye. Coastal trails accessible from Mallaig.
- **Settle → Carlisle**: Stop at Ribblehead for viaduct walk; lunch in Hawes. Continue to Carlisle in evening for overnight.

This map approach allows flexibility and ensures that every stop is optimized for scenery, comfort, and cultural immersion.

Planning your scenic train journey through Britain is an art of balancing routes, seasons, connections, and local experiences. Focus on landscapes that inspire you, cultural stops that intrigue you, and comfort that allows you to enjoy the ride. Proper preparation transforms a simple train trip into an unforgettable adventure—one where every window frame frames a memory.

ESSENTIAL TRAVEL TIPS FOR TRAIN EXPLORERS

Exploring Britain by train is one of the most rewarding ways to experience the country. From bustling cities to remote coastal villages, the rail network offers unparalleled access to both iconic sights and hidden gems. However, to truly enjoy your journey, a little preparation and insider knowledge can make a significant difference. This section will equip you with practical guidance on planning, navigating, and savoring Britain's rail adventures.

Train Travel Essentail

PLANNING YOUR TRAIN JOURNEY

Booking and Tickets

Britain's rail system is extensive, but fares vary widely depending on timing, route, and train operator. Tickets can be booked up to 12 weeks in advance for most services. For the best value:

- **Advance Tickets:** Ideal for long-distance journeys, these are non-refundable but often significantly cheaper than buying on the day.

- **Railcards:** If you are over 60, a student, traveling as a group, or under 26, railcards provide up to a third off ticket prices.
- **Flexible Options:** For spontaneous exploration, consider an *Anytime* or *Off-Peak* ticket. Off-Peak tickets avoid busy commuter times, usually after 9:30 a.m. on weekdays.
- **BritRail Passes:** For international travelers, these passes offer unlimited travel for a set number of days across England, Scotland, and Wales, perfect for hopping between cities without the stress of individual tickets.

Apps and Timetables

- **National Rail Enquiries:** The official website and app provide real-time train times, delays, platform changes, and connections.
- **Trainline App:** Convenient for booking, mobile tickets, and tracking multiple operators.
- **Local Operators:** Some scenic routes, like the Settle-Carlisle or West Highland Line, are operated by specific companies (e.g., Northern Rail, ScotRail). Check their websites for seasonal services and reservations.

Packing and Travel Essentials

Luggage

Train travel in Britain is comfortable, but space can be limited on regional and heritage lines. Pack light and compact:

- Rolling suitcases fit in overhead racks; smaller backpacks can be stored under your seat.
- For long journeys, consider a small daypack for essentials like water, snacks, a camera, and a rain jacket.

Clothing

Weather in Britain is famously changeable, even in summer. Layering is essential:

- Waterproof jacket and sturdy walking shoes for countryside exploration.
- Scarves or hats for winter journeys through the Highlands or northern England.

- Comfortable clothing for long train rides; seats on intercity trains are generous, but older regional trains may be less spacious.

Tech and Connectivity

- Wi-Fi is increasingly available on intercity trains but less reliable on rural routes. Download maps and entertainment beforehand.
- Power sockets are standard on modern intercity trains; bring a portable charger for regional lines.

NAVIGATING STATIONS AND TRANSFERS

Major Hubs

Britain's train network revolves around major city stations:

- **London:** King's Cross (northbound), Paddington (westbound), Victoria (south coast), Euston (northwest), Liverpool Street (east). Each station has clear signage and facilities including left luggage, cafes, and rail information desks.
- **Edinburgh Waverley & Glasgow Central:** Gateways to Scotland's scenic lines. Both stations are within walking distance of city centers.
- **Manchester Piccadilly & Birmingham New Street:** Central points for north-south and regional connections.

Transfers

- Connections between trains in large cities often require walking between platforms or even across stations. Allow at least 15–20 minutes for transfers in London and 10–15 minutes in smaller hubs.
- Many stations are integrated with bus, tram, or subway services. For example, Manchester has a MetroLink tram stop connected to Piccadilly, ideal for reaching suburbs or nearby attractions.

Onboard Comfort and Experience

Seating

- **Standard Class:** Comfortable for day trips, with fold-down tables and power sockets on modern trains.

- **First Class:** Wider seats, quieter cars, complimentary refreshments on long routes. Ideal for scenic journeys or working on the go.
- **Window Seats:** For scenic lines, always aim for a window seat. Northern routes like the West Highland Line or Heart of Wales Line offer stunning landscapes; book early as these seats are in high demand.

Dining

- Many intercity trains have snack bars or trolley services offering sandwiches, hot drinks, and light meals.
- On long scenic routes, pack local specialties to enjoy onboard. For instance, Cornish pasties for a southwest train or Scottish shortbread on Highland services.

EXPERIENCING THE SCENERY

Iconic Routes

Mallaig Western Highlands

Some of Britain's most scenic rail journeys are highlights themselves:

- **West Highland Line (Glasgow to Mallaig):** Rugged mountains, Loch Lomond, and the iconic Glenfinnan Viaduct. Best in spring or autumn for dramatic landscapes.

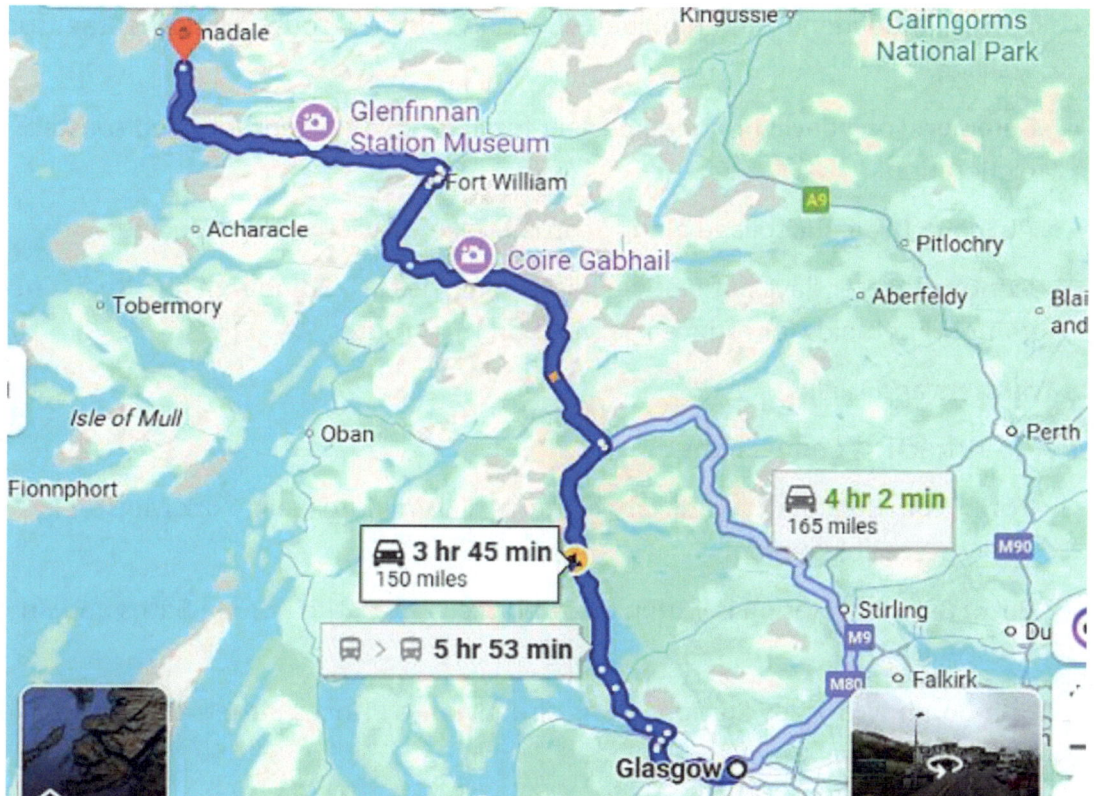

Glasgow to Mallaig train route

- **Settle-Carlisle Line (Yorkshire to Cumbria):** Sweeping valleys, limestone bridges, and traditional market towns. Early morning trains offer soft light for photography.
- **Heart of Wales Line (Shrewsbury to Swansea):** Remote hills, charming villages, and rarely crowded carriages. Ideal for a quiet escape.

Hidden Gems

- **Severn Valley Railway:** A heritage line in Worcestershire, perfect for families and steam enthusiasts.
- **Bristol to Bath:** A short but picturesque regional route through rolling West Country hills.

- **Isle of Wight Steam Railway:** For those combining trains with coastal exploration.

Seasonal Considerations

- **Spring:** Rhododendrons and bluebells along southern routes; mild weather for walking.
- **Summer:** Long daylight hours; perfect for extended rail journeys and coastal exploration.
- **Autumn:** Dramatic foliage along Scottish, Lake District, and Welsh lines.
- **Winter:** Shorter days but festive markets in cities like Edinburgh and York. Check winter timetables for reduced services on rural routes.

Local Transfers and Walks

Station-to-Attraction Connections

- **York:** From York Station, the city center is a 10-minute walk; York Minster is easily accessible on foot.
- **Bath:** Bath Spa Station is within a 15-minute walk to the Roman Baths and Royal Crescent.
- **Edinburgh:** Waverley Station opens directly onto Princes Street; the Royal Mile is a 5-minute stroll.

Combining Rail and Bus

Some destinations require a short bus ride:

- **Snowdonia:** From Bangor Station, take the 75 or 76 bus to Llanberis for hiking routes and mountain railways.
- **Lake District:** Windermere Station connects via Stagecoach buses to villages like Ambleside and Grasmere.

CULTURAL INSIGHTS FOR RAIL TRAVELERS

Regional Etiquette

- Punctuality is valued. Trains run to strict timetables; always arrive a few minutes early.

- Quiet zones are enforced on many long-distance trains. Keep phone calls minimal and use headphones.
- Tipping is not customary on trains but appreciated in onboard dining cars.

Local Food Highlights

- **Scotland:** Try a freshly baked "Cullen Skink" soup in Inverness before boarding.
- **Cornwall:** Grab a pasty from Penzance for the journey along the coast.
- **Yorkshire:** A slice of Parkin cake or locally brewed ale makes a scenic pitstop more memorable.

Safety and Practical Tips

- Keep your belongings close, especially on busy commuter routes.
- Use station lockers for day trips if you plan to explore without luggage.
- For remote lines, carry water and snacks; small stations may have limited facilities.
- Always check the return timetable, especially in rural areas where evening services may be infrequent.

Maximizing the Train Experience

- **Scenic Planning:** Identify window-side highlights beforehand using route maps; many scenic lines have dedicated commentary on board or via apps.
- **Local Exploration:** Plan stops mid-route to explore towns or countryside. For example, disembark at Fort William for a Loch Ness detour.
- **Photographic Opportunities:** Early morning or late afternoon light offers the most dramatic landscapes; have your camera ready.
- **Relaxation:** Don't rush. One of the joys of train travel is the pace itself, letting you watch the countryside unfold without stress.

Train travel in Britain is about more than transportation—it's a journey through culture, landscapes, and history. By planning ahead, packing thoughtfully, and embracing the local rhythm, every route becomes an adventure. From the vibrant energy of London's hubs to the quiet charm of remote rural lines, these tips ensure your rail exploration is smooth, scenic, and unforgettable.

CHAPTER 2
SOUTHERN ENGLAND: CASTLES, COASTLINES & HISTORY

Southern England is a region where the past and present blend seamlessly. From its grand castles perched on dramatic hilltops to its picturesque coastlines and historic cities, this area offers some of the UK's most captivating destinations, all easily accessible by train. Whether you're a history enthusiast, a nature lover, or a seeker of seaside charm, traveling through Southern England by rail provides an immersive and convenient way to explore its many wonders.

Southern England train route

In this section, we'll explore the best train routes in Southern England, highlighting castles, coastal villages, ancient cities, and charming countryside. We'll cover must-see destinations, practical tips for your journey, and insider advice on how to make the most of your trip to this vibrant and diverse part of Britain.

Exploring the South: An Overview of Southern England by Rail

Southern England is known for its beautiful landscapes, historical landmarks, and easy rail connectivity. From London's bustling streets to the tranquil hills of the Cotswolds, trains provide an excellent way to explore the region's scenic beauty and cultural richness.

The train network in Southern England is efficient, with regular services to major cities and tourist hotspots. Whether you're traveling from London to the seaside towns of Cornwall or heading to historic Bath or Oxford, the train system makes it simple to access the region's highlights. In addition to the convenience, the train journeys themselves offer scenic views, from rolling countryside to breathtaking coastlines.

KEY TRAIN ROUTES IN SOUTHERN ENGLAND

London to Bath: History & Georgian Elegance

A direct train ride from London to Bath offers a chance to experience two sides of England—London's modern buzz and Bath's historic, Georgian charm. The journey from London Paddington to Bath Spa takes about 1 hour 30 minutes, passing through beautiful countryside.

Georgian Elegance top view

- **Highlights**: Once in Bath, you'll find the famous Roman Baths, a UNESCO World Heritage site, and the elegant Georgian architecture, including the stunning Royal Crescent. Don't miss a stroll along the River Avon and a visit to the Jane Austen Centre for a glimpse into the life of one of England's most beloved authors.

- **Local Transfer**: Bath is a compact city and easily explored on foot. If you're venturing out to the surrounding countryside, buses and taxis are available to visit nearby attractions like the charming village of Lacock or the historic Stonehenge.

- **When to Go**: Spring and autumn are ideal for visiting Bath, with the city's gardens in full bloom and fewer tourists. Summer can be crowded, but the festivals and events make it a vibrant time to visit.

London to Oxford: Academic Excellence & Riverside Charm

Oxford, one of the world's most famous academic cities, is just a short 1-hour train ride from London. The route, departing from Paddington Station, offers picturesque views of the English countryside.

- **Highlights**: Oxford is known for its stunning architecture, particularly the ancient colleges of the University of Oxford. Visitors can explore iconic landmarks like the Bodleian Library, the Ashmolean Museum, and Christ Church College. The nearby countryside offers plenty of walking trails, including those along the Thames Path.

- **Local Transfer**: Oxford is easy to navigate on foot, but if you're looking to explore nearby villages, local buses and bike hire options are readily available. For a relaxing river cruise, take a boat ride along the River Thames to explore Oxford's picturesque waterside.

- **When to Go**: Oxford is lovely year-round, but if you're interested in the city's academic atmosphere, aim to visit during term time in autumn or spring.

London to Brighton: Seaside Glamour & Pier Fun

Brighton, with its eclectic charm and lively atmosphere, is one of the most popular coastal destinations in the south. A 1-hour train ride from London Victoria Station takes you to this iconic seaside city, where the relaxed pace of life contrasts with London's energy.

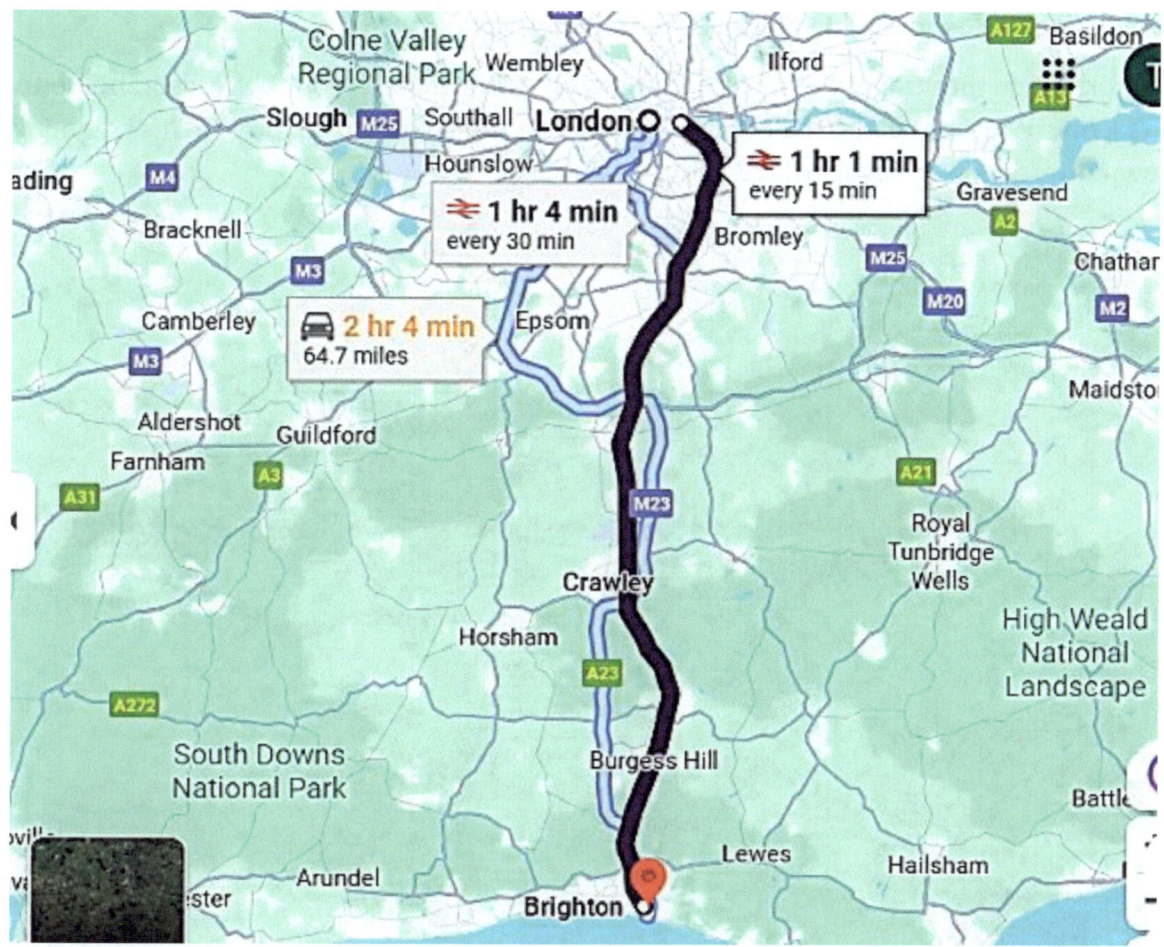

London to Brighton train route

- **Highlights**: Once you arrive in Brighton, head straight for the iconic Brighton Pier, which has been a staple of seaside fun for generations. Explore the famous Royal Pavilion, a palace with an exotic, Indian-inspired architecture, or wander through the Lanes, a maze of narrow streets filled with boutique shops, cafes, and independent stores.

- **Local Transfer**: Brighton is compact, and most attractions are within walking distance of the train station. For a scenic walk, take the coastal path to nearby Hove, or ride a local bus to visit the tranquil Preston Park.

- **When to Go**: Summer is the best time to enjoy Brighton's vibrant atmosphere and beautiful beaches, though it can be crowded. For a quieter experience, visit in spring or early autumn.

London to Windsor: Royal Palaces & Picturesque Towns

A short 30-minute train ride from London Paddington will take you to Windsor, home to the iconic Windsor Castle, the official residence of the British royal family. This charming town offers a mix of royal history and quaint riverside beauty.

- **Highlights**: The primary draw is Windsor Castle, where you can explore the State Apartments, St. George's Chapel, and the lovely castle grounds. Afterward, take a stroll along the River Thames or visit the quaint shops and cafes in Windsor's town center.

- **Local Transfer**: Windsor is small, and most attractions are within walking distance. To get to the nearby Windsor Great Park, you can take a local bus or a leisurely walk from the castle.

- **When to Go**: Windsor is best enjoyed in spring or autumn when the crowds are thinner and the castle grounds are at their most picturesque. Summer offers additional events, but it can get crowded, especially around the castle.

London to Salisbury: Cathedrals & Stone Circles

Salisbury, famous for its stunning cathedral and proximity to the prehistoric monument of Stonehenge, is easily accessible from London in just 1 hour 30 minutes. Trains depart from London Waterloo Station.

- **Highlights**: Salisbury Cathedral, home to the tallest spire in Britain, is a must-visit. The cathedral's stunning architecture and medieval history are complemented by its serene setting. Don't miss a trip to the nearby Stonehenge, one of the world's most famous and mysterious landmarks.

- **Local Transfer**: Salisbury is small and can easily be explored on foot. If you want to reach Stonehenge, buses operate regularly from Salisbury to the site. Alternatively, take a guided tour that includes transport and insight into the history of the monument.

- **When to Go**: Summer is the most popular time to visit Stonehenge, but it can get busy. Spring and autumn are quieter, and the weather is still pleasant.

HIDDEN GEMS IN SOUTHERN ENGLAND

While the well-known attractions of Southern England are certainly worth a visit, there are also a number of hidden gems that can be easily accessed by rail.

The Isle of Wight: Seaside Serenity & Victorian Charm

The Isle of Wight is a picturesque island off the southern coast of England, known for its sandy beaches, charming villages, and historical sites. You can reach it by train to Portsmouth, followed by a short ferry ride to the island.

- **Highlights**: Visit the Victorian seaside resort of Shanklin, explore the beautiful Osborne House, and walk along the island's coastal paths with stunning sea views.

- **When to Go**: Spring and early summer are perfect for visiting the Isle of Wight, as the weather is mild, and the island's flower-filled landscapes are at their best.

The Cotswolds: English Countryside at Its Best

The Cotswolds, a region of rolling hills, charming villages, and historic market towns, can be reached by train from London Paddington to Moreton-in-Marsh, with additional local transport available to explore the area.

The Cotswolds scenic view

- **Highlights**: Wander through the picturesque villages of Bourton-on-the-Water, Stow-on-the-Wold, and Chipping Campden. The Cotswold Way, a long-distance walking path, offers magnificent views of the surrounding countryside.
- **When to Go**: The Cotswolds is stunning year-round, but it's particularly beautiful in spring and summer, when the countryside is in full bloom.

Southern England is a treasure trove of historical landmarks, beautiful coastlines, and charming towns, all of which are easily accessible by train. Whether you're visiting royal residences like Windsor Castle, wandering through the streets of Bath, or soaking up the atmosphere of Brighton, each destination offers a unique experience. Trains provide a perfect way to connect with these places, offering comfort, ease, and breathtaking views along the way.

With careful planning, you can make the most of your rail adventure through Southern England—discovering not only iconic landmarks but also hidden gems that showcase the region's true beauty. So, hop on the train and let the journey begin!

BATH TO BRIGHTON: A GEORGIAN & SEASIDE ADVENTURE

Traveling by train from **Bath to Brighton** is a journey that beautifully combines Britain's elegant Georgian architecture with the vibrant charm of its southern seaside. This route covers about 150 miles across the West and South of England, linking historic cities, charming market towns, and the iconic southern coast. Perfect for a day trip or a weekend getaway, the journey showcases diverse scenery, from rolling Cotswold hills to the chalk cliffs of Sussex.

Bath to Brighton train route atlas

GETTING THERE: TRAIN CONNECTIONS & TIMING

The journey from **Bath Spa Station** to **Brighton Station** typically takes **around 2 hours 30 minutes to 3 hours**, depending on transfers. There are no direct trains for most of the day, so travelers should plan a change, usually at **Bristol Temple Meads** or **London Paddington/London Victoria**.

- **Route Option 1 (via Bristol & London):** Bath Spa → Bristol Temple Meads → London Paddington → London Victoria → Brighton. This takes slightly longer but offers high-speed connections and comfortable services on GWR and Southern Rail.

- **Route Option 2 (via Reading):** Bath Spa → Reading → Brighton. This route avoids central London transfers and is practical for those who prefer less crowded lines.

Train Operators:

- **Great Western Railway (GWR):** Bath Spa to Reading/Bristol and London. Fast, modern intercity trains with Wi-Fi and refreshments.
- **Southern Rail:** London Victoria or Gatwick to Brighton. Known for coastal views and frequent services.
- **Thameslink:** Provides some direct services from Gatwick/London Bridge to Brighton, helpful for seamless transfers.

Tips:

- Off-peak tickets are cheaper, and advance booking can save up to 50%.
- Seat reservations on intercity trains are recommended, especially during summer weekends.
- Bring a compact umbrella—southern England weather is famously changeable.

Bath: Georgian Splendor

Bath Spa Station is centrally located, just a 10–15-minute walk from the city center. Bath is famous for its **Georgian architecture**, Roman baths, and elegant streets. Key highlights include:

- **The Roman Baths & Pump Room:** Explore ancient Roman ruins and enjoy the spa water. The Pump Room restaurant offers a historic ambiance and traditional afternoon tea.
- **Royal Crescent & The Circus:** Iconic curved terraces of Georgian architecture, perfect for photography.
- **Pulteney Bridge:** A historic bridge lined with shops, crossing the River Avon.

On Foot: Bath's compact city center is best explored on foot. Walking along the **Avon River Path** offers scenic views of the city's skyline.

Food & Drink:

- **Sally Lunn's Historic Eating House:** Famous for its Bath bun, a sweet, soft bread that's perfect with tea.
- **The Raven:** Traditional pub serving hearty British fare, ideal for a mid-morning stop before catching your train south.

Seasonal Tip: Spring and early summer are ideal, as the gardens bloom along the Royal Crescent, and outdoor terraces are pleasant for tea or lunch.

En Route: The Countryside Between Bath and Brighton

The journey south passes through **Somerset, Wiltshire, and West Sussex**, offering rolling hills, market towns, and river valleys. Notable stops worth a short detour include:

- **Salisbury:** Famous for its medieval cathedral with the tallest spire in England and nearby Stonehenge. Salisbury Station is a short walk to the historic center.
- **Winchester:** A historic city with a grand cathedral and charming streets. Ideal for a coffee stop or quick exploration.
- **Arundel:** A small market town with a restored castle overlooking the River Arun. From the station, it's a 10-minute walk into town.

Scenic Insight: Windows on the southern route reveal lush pastures and hedgerows. In autumn, the trees in Hampshire and West Sussex turn brilliant gold and crimson, making the train ride especially picturesque.

Food Tip for Onboard: Pick up a Cornish pasty from Bath Spa station for a filling, traditional snack during the journey.

Brighton: Coastal Vibrancy & Cultural Highlights

Brighton Station opens onto a lively city known for its arts, nightlife, and seafront charm. The station is centrally located, just 10 minutes' walk to the **Brighton Palace Pier**.

Seafront & Pier:

- Walk along the pebbled beach to **Brighton Palace Pier**, which has amusement rides, arcades, and food stalls.
- **Brighton Beach Huts:** Iconic, colorful huts ideal for photos. Early morning or late afternoon light is perfect for photography.

Brighton Beach | Iconic Seaside Destination

The Lanes:

- A network of narrow, winding streets with independent shops, cafes, and galleries. Handmade jewelry, vintage clothing, and antiques are highlights.
- **Food & Drink:** Try fish and chips from **The Regency Restaurant**, or enjoy gourmet coffee and pastries at **Café Coho**.

Royal Pavilion:

- A must-see for its extravagant Indo-Saracenic architecture and interior design. Walking from the station takes around 20 minutes, or take a short taxi ride.

Cultural Insight: Brighton is famous for its **arts and LGBTQ+ culture**, with vibrant events year-round, including the Brighton Festival in May and the Brighton Pride Parade in August.

Seasonal Tips:

- Summer: Beach and pier are lively but crowded.
- Spring & Autumn: Quieter, pleasant weather for walking and photography.
- Winter: Seaside promenades are windswept but magical; pubs and cafés are cozy refuges.

SUGGESTED DAY TRIP OR SHORT BREAK

Day Trip Option:

- Depart Bath early morning, explore the Roman Baths and Royal Crescent, then board a late-morning train toward Brighton.
- Stop in Winchester or Arundel for lunch and a short exploration.
- Arrive in Brighton mid-afternoon, explore the seafront, The Lanes, and the Royal Pavilion. Enjoy dinner before returning to Bath by evening train.

Weekend Option:

- Overnight in Brighton at a seafront hotel like **The Grand Brighton** or a boutique guesthouse in The Lanes.
- Spend a full day visiting Brighton's museums, art galleries, or take a short bus to nearby **South Downs National Park** for hiking.

Local Transfer Insight:

- Brighton's city buses cover most local attractions if walking isn't convenient.
- For trips to the South Downs, taxis or guided tours from Brighton are efficient.

Practical Travel Tips

- **Booking Tickets:** Use National Rail or Trainline apps. Booking 2–3 weeks in advance secures better fares.
- **Luggage:** Both Bath and Brighton stations have luggage storage. Compact backpacks are recommended for day trips.
- **Connectivity:** Free Wi-Fi is available on most intercity trains, making it easy to plan stops or check maps en route.
- **Accessibility:** Both Bath Spa and Brighton stations are wheelchair-friendly, with lifts and step-free access.

Cultural Etiquette:

- Punctuality is appreciated in the UK. Trains usually depart on time, and delays are promptly announced.
- Polite behavior on trains and in cafes/pubs enhances the experience. British pubs often operate a "table service" system for food.

Personal Insight

Having traveled this route multiple times, I recommend **window seats on the left side of southbound trains** for the best countryside views between Bath and Arundel. The rolling hills, hedgerows, and river valleys in Hampshire are subtle but enchanting. Brighton itself feels like two worlds: the urban creativity of the city center, and the relaxed seaside vibe along the promenade. Combining the historic elegance of Bath with the lively southern coast creates a perfectly balanced adventure for history buffs, food lovers, and seaside enthusiasts alike.

Tip: Take your time. The journey isn't just about the start and end points; the towns in between offer hidden gems, from local bakeries to small art galleries that are easy to miss if rushing.

The **Bath to Brighton** rail journey is a classic British adventure, linking the refined Georgian elegance of Bath with the colorful seaside culture of Brighton. The combination of scenic countryside, historic towns, and vibrant coastal life makes it perfect for a single day trip or a leisurely weekend. With careful planning, off-peak tickets, and attention to seasonal highlights, travelers can enjoy every stop, from historic cathedrals to colorful beach huts, all accessible by Britain's well-connected and comfortable rail network.

EXPLORING STONEHENGE FROM SALISBURY BY RAIL

Visiting Stonehenge, one of Britain's most iconic prehistoric monuments, is surprisingly easy and rewarding when approached by rail. Traveling by train allows you to avoid the traffic, enjoy the English countryside, and explore Salisbury—a historic city that pairs beautifully with the world-famous stone circle. This guide provides a complete, practical roadmap for a smooth, scenic, and culturally rich journey.

GETTING TO SALISBURY BY TRAIN

Salisbury is well connected to London and other major cities, making it a perfect rail gateway to Stonehenge.

- **From London:** Direct trains depart from London Waterloo to Salisbury approximately every 30 minutes. The journey takes about 90 minutes. Trains are operated by South Western Railway, offering both first-class and standard seating. The line passes through rolling Wiltshire countryside and small market towns, offering a gentle introduction to southern England.

- **From Exeter or Bristol:** Great Western Railway and CrossCountry trains connect via Salisbury, with a change at Southampton or Westbury depending on the route.
- **From Bath:** Trains run through Westbury, with scenic views of the Avon valley and surrounding farmland.

Visit Stonehenge and Salisbury

Tip: Book tickets in advance for cheaper fares. Window seats on the left side traveling from London offer glimpses of the meadows and woodland typical of Wiltshire.

Salisbury Station to the City Center

Salisbury railway station is compact, easy to navigate, and only a short walk from the city center:

- Exit the station and turn right onto Fisherton Street. A 15-minute walk brings you to the medieval heart of Salisbury.
- Alternatively, frequent buses and taxis can take you into the city center in under 5 minutes, ideal for those carrying luggage or with limited mobility.

Insight: Walking allows you to notice charming shops and historic buildings along the way, including traditional pubs and small cafés that serve locally baked pastries.

Exploring Salisbury Before Stonehenge

Salisbury is rich in history and architecture, and a morning or afternoon visit enhances your Stonehenge experience:

- **Salisbury Cathedral:** A must-see, home to the tallest spire in Britain and one of the four surviving original Magna Carta manuscripts. Admission includes the cathedral close and often a guided tour.

- **Market Square:** Traditional stalls sell local produce, crafts, and antiques. Seasonal specialties such as Wiltshire cheeses, cider, and fresh flowers make excellent picnic supplies for your Stonehenge visit.

- **Arundells (Salisbury Museum):** Offers insights into the life of former Prime Minister Edward Heath and local history exhibits, perfect for understanding the region's cultural context.

Practical Tip: Plan at least 2–3 hours in Salisbury before heading to Stonehenge, both for sightseeing and to pick up any provisions.

GETTING TO STONEHENGE FROM SALISBURY

Stonehenge is 9 miles northwest of Salisbury. Public transport options make it convenient without a car:

- **By Bus:** The Stonehenge Tour Bus (operated by the National Trust) departs from Salisbury Bus Station near the train station. It runs every 30–60 minutes and includes a combined ticket with Stonehenge entry. The journey takes approximately 30 minutes.

- **By Bicycle:** For adventurous travelers, hire a bike from Salisbury city center. The ride is scenic along country lanes with views of chalk downs and farmland. It takes roughly 45–60 minutes each way.

- **By Taxi or Rideshare:** Quickest option for those short on time, taking 20–25 minutes.

Personal Insight: Taking the official tour bus is highly recommended. It avoids parking congestion, drops you close to the visitor center, and provides informative commentary en route.

Stonehenge Visitor Center

The modern visitor center is 2 miles from the stone circle and offers extensive context for your visit:

- **Exhibits:** Archaeological finds, interactive displays, and digital reconstructions explain the history, construction, and mystery of the stones.
- **Amenities:** Café serving hot meals and local snacks, a gift shop with books and handcrafted souvenirs, restrooms, and picnic areas.
- **Ticketing:** Entry is timed; booking online in advance ensures your preferred slot, especially in summer or on weekends.

Tip: Arrive 30 minutes before your entry time to explore the visitor center exhibits—it enriches the experience of seeing the stones.

Experiencing the Stone Circle

The walk from the visitor center to the stones is about 10–15 minutes along a flat, gravel path with clear directional signage:

- **Viewing Options:** The main path takes you to the circle's perimeter. For photography, morning or late afternoon light provides dramatic shadows.
- **Audio Guide:** Available for download, giving historical context, theories, and folklore.
- **Accessibility:** Wheelchair-accessible paths exist from the visitor center, although terrain around the stones is uneven.

Pro Tip: Don't rush the visit. Walking the perimeter slowly allows observation of the stones' alignment with the solstices and appreciation of the surrounding landscape of Salisbury Plain.

Combining Nearby Attractions

Salisbury Plain and surrounding areas offer additional points of interest for a full-day excursion:

- **Old Sarum:** A 15-minute drive or 30-minute cycle from Salisbury, this Iron Age hillfort overlooks the plain and provides historical context for Stonehenge.

- **Avebury Stone Circle:** Slightly farther afield but reachable by train and bus from Swindon or direct tour, offering a contrasting stone circle experience in a village setting.
- **Wilton House:** 5 miles west of Salisbury, reachable by bus or taxi, a stately home with gardens and exhibitions, often used as a filming location.

Insider Tip: Combining Stonehenge with Old Sarum in one day offers a sense of ancient Britain from different perspectives—fortress and ritual landscape.

Food and Refreshments

Good food options are available before, during, and after your visit:

- **Salisbury:** Try local specialties such as Wiltshire cured meats, cream teas, or hearty pies at cafés like The Chapter House near the cathedral.
- **Stonehenge Visitor Center Café:** Soups, sandwiches, and light meals sourced locally. Perfect for a mid-visit refresh.
- **Picnics:** Seasonal produce from Salisbury Market makes a scenic picnic by the visitor center's outdoor seating area.

Pro Tip: Bring a refillable water bottle; walking around Salisbury Plain can be surprisingly dehydrating on sunny days.

Seasonal Considerations

Timing your visit can affect the experience:

- **Spring (March–May):** Mild weather, fewer crowds, wildflowers bloom on Salisbury Plain.
- **Summer (June–August):** Long days, busy visitor center. Advance booking is essential; solstice events are particularly popular.
- **Autumn (September–November):** Dramatic skies, golden fields; ideal for photography.
- **Winter (December–February):** Crisp air, fewer tourists; the stones appear more atmospheric against misty skies.

Travel Insight: Sunrise and sunset visits offer unique lighting for photography, especially in autumn and winter. The visitor center is closed early in winter, so plan accordingly.

Returning to Salisbury and Beyond

After visiting Stonehenge:

- **Return by Bus:** The same National Trust tour bus runs back to Salisbury city center, coordinating with train schedules.
- **Walking or Cycling:** Optional for those who started by bike; enjoy scenic lanes back into the city.
- **Further Travel:** Salisbury connects by rail to London, Bath, and the South Coast. Many travelers continue to Winchester or Exeter for additional historic towns along the route.

Practical Tip: Give yourself at least 1–2 hours to explore Salisbury before catching your return train, as the city itself deserves attention beyond just Stonehenge.

Summary Travel Map (Rail and Local Transfers)

- **Step 1:** Train from London Waterloo → Salisbury (90 min).
- **Step 2:** Walk 15 min or take a short bus/taxi ride → Salisbury city center. Optional sightseeing: Cathedral, Market Square, Arundells.
- **Step 3:** National Trust Stonehenge Tour Bus (30 min) → Stonehenge Visitor Center.
- **Step 4:** 10–15 min walk → Stone Circle. Optional nearby visit: Old Sarum (bus/taxi/ bike).
- **Step 5:** Return to Salisbury via bus/taxi. Evening train back to London or onward destination.

This sequence balances convenience, sightseeing, and local immersion.

Personal Insight

Traveling to Stonehenge by train allows a calm, scenic introduction to southern England. Unlike driving, the journey emphasizes the countryside and historical towns, with Salisbury providing a cultural anchor. Taking the bus from Salisbury to the site avoids parking stress and offers commentary along the way. Combining city exploration, local food, and ancient monuments makes this a satisfying and practical day trip.

HIDDEN VILLAGES AND SEASIDE ESCAPES ON THE SOUTH COAST

Britain's South Coast offers some of the country's most picturesque and often overlooked destinations. Beyond the busy seaside towns, there are quiet fishing villages, dramatic cliffs, and historic harbors that are perfectly accessible by train. This section guides you through these hidden gems, with practical directions, seasonal tips, cultural insights, and local culinary highlights.

South West England

PLANNING YOUR SOUTH COAST JOURNEY

Train Connections

The South Coast is served by a mix of regional and intercity rail lines:

- **Southern Rail** connects London with Brighton, Hastings, Eastbourne, and Portsmouth.
- **South Western Railway** serves the western South Coast, including Bournemouth, Weymouth, and Southampton.
- **Great Western Railway** provides access to Dorset's coast, including Dorchester, Weymouth, and Poole.

For scenic and less-traveled routes, regional lines are ideal. Booking in advance is recommended for summer weekends when coastal trains are busy, especially to small stations like Seaford or Beer.

Best Time to Travel

- **Spring (March–May):** Mild temperatures, blooming gardens, fewer tourists.
- **Summer (June–August):** Ideal for swimming and coastal walks, but expect crowded trains and higher accommodation costs.
- **Autumn (September–October):** Coastal walks are quieter, with dramatic sunsets and golden light over cliffs.
- **Winter (November–February):** Off-season charm, perfect for storm-watching and cozy pubs, though some local attractions may close.

HIDDEN VILLAGES WORTH THE JOURNEY

Alfriston, East Sussex

- **Access:** Take Southern Rail to Polegate, then a short 15-minute taxi or local bus to Alfriston.
- **Highlights:** Known as the "gateway to the South Downs," Alfriston is a quintessential English village with flint cottages, narrow streets, and the historic Clergy House. Walking trails through the Downs are easily accessible from the village.
- **Insider Tip:** Walk the 3-mile trail from Alfriston to the Seven Sisters cliffs for dramatic chalk landscapes. Take a packed lunch and enjoy the panoramic views.

Beer, Devon

- **Access:** Train to Seaton or Axminster, then a 10-minute local bus ride. Beer itself has no station, keeping it delightfully quiet.
- **Highlights:** This fishing village is famous for its pebble beach, historic caves, and quaint harbor. Beer's limestone cliffs are ideal for gentle hiking or rock climbing.
- **Culinary Note:** Sample locally brewed Beer Ale in the village pubs and freshly caught seafood at the harbor.

Lymington, Hampshire

- **Access:** South Western Railway from London Waterloo to Brockenhurst, then a connecting train or taxi to Lymington Town station.
- **Highlights:** Lymington is a port town with cobbled streets, Georgian architecture, and a ferry service to the Isle of Wight. Its salt marshes are excellent for birdwatching.
- **Seasonal Tip:** Visit in summer for the bustling marina; autumn offers quieter walks along the Solent shore.

Lymington

Seaside Escapes for Relaxation

Sidmouth, Devon

- **Access:** Take GWR to Exeter St Davids, then a scenic bus through Devon's countryside (around 1 hour).
- **Highlights:** Sidmouth boasts a Regency promenade, pebble beach, and lush gardens. The nearby Jurassic Coast offers fossil-hunting opportunities and cliff-top walks.

- **Insider Tip:** The Sid Vale Association maintains walking routes with informative plaques about local wildlife and history.

Hastings Old Town, East Sussex

- **Access:** Southern Rail from London Charing Cross or London Victoria directly to Hastings Station, then a 10-minute walk to the Old Town.
- **Highlights:** Narrow streets lined with independent shops, seafood restaurants, and the famous Hastings Pier. For history lovers, the Hastings Castle ruins are a short uphill walk.
- **Culinary Note:** Try the local specialty, "Hastings Rock" candy, and fresh fish from the harbor.

Mevagissey, Cornwall

- **Access:** Train to St Austell on GWR, then take a 25-minute bus ride or taxi.
- **Highlights:** This small fishing village offers a picturesque harbor, art galleries, and cozy pubs. The surrounding South West Coast Path provides breathtaking cliff-top views.
- **Seasonal Tip:** Spring and summer are ideal for boat trips to spot seals and seabirds.

SCENIC COASTAL ROUTES BY TRAIN

Eastbourne to Seaford

- **Route:** Southern Rail, a short 20-minute journey along the coast.
- **Highlights:** Stunning views of the Seven Sisters chalk cliffs and rolling South Downs. The walk from Seaford Station to the cliffs is a gentle 15-minute hike through farmland.
- **Experience Insight:** Sitting on the left side of the train offers the best views of the cliffs and sea.

Eastbourne to Seaford scenic route

Exeter to Lyme Regis

- **Route:** GWR to Axminster, then a connecting bus to Lyme Regis.

- **Highlights:** A historic market town with fossil-rich beaches. The Cobb harbor is famous from film and literature.

- **Insider Tip:** Walk along the Jurassic Coast Path early in the morning to enjoy quiet beaches and sunrise over the bay.

Exeter to Lyme Regis train route

Brighton to Hastings via Eastbourne

- **Route:** Southern Rail offers a direct line along the coast.
- **Highlights:** Between Eastbourne and Hastings, the train skirts chalk cliffs, hidden coves, and seaside towns.
- **Experience Insight:** Plan a stop in Eastbourne to walk the pier and explore the Victorian promenade before continuing to Hastings.

Cultural Highlights Along the Coast

Historic Architecture

- Many villages retain their original character with flint cottages, Tudor-era buildings, and Georgian terraces. Alfriston's Clergy House is England's first National Trust property, while Lymington's High Street boasts Georgian facades with antique shops.

Local Festivals

- **Sidmouth Folk Festival (July):** Traditional music, dance, and crafts.
- **Hastings Seafood & Wine Festival (May):** Celebrate local flavors right on the harbor.
- **Beer & Music Festival (August):** Live music alongside local seafood and ales.

Maritime Heritage

- Museums, piers, and preserved harbors reveal the South Coast's seafaring history. The Shipwreck Museum in Hastings and the Cobb in Lyme Regis are small but rich with stories.

Food and Drink on the South Coast

Seafood Specialties

- Many villages serve freshly caught fish and shellfish. Look for local specialties:
    - **Hastings:** Smoked mackerel or kippers.
    - **Beer:** Crab and lobster dishes at the harbor pubs.
    - **Sidmouth:** Freshly baked pasties with Devon cream teas.

Local Drinks

- Craft ales, local ciders, and wines from Sussex vineyards enhance the coastal experience. Many pubs source ingredients from nearby farms, ensuring authenticity and freshness.

Seasonal Markets

- Weekly farmers' markets offer local produce and handmade goods. Brighton, Lewes, and St Ives are great stops if your itinerary allows.

WALKING AND EXPLORATION TIPS

Cliff and Coastal Walks

- Always wear sturdy shoes, as cliff paths can be uneven and slippery after rain.
- Check tide times when walking along pebble or sandy beaches. Some coastal paths require a short inland detour during high tides.

Village Exploration

- Start at the train station and explore on foot. Most villages are compact, with key attractions, pubs, and shops within a 10–15-minute walk.
- Follow local signposts for walking trails; many provide historical or natural context along the way.

Photography Tips

- Early morning light on the coast provides soft, dramatic scenes.
- Bring a polarizing filter or smartphone lens attachment to reduce glare on water and enhance cliff textures.

Local Transfers and Accessibility

- **Buses:** Many villages are reachable by short bus rides from nearby stations. South West Coaches, Stagecoach, and local operators run regular services.
- **Taxis:** Convenient for late arrivals or to reach less accessible villages like Beer or Mevagissey.
- **On Foot:** Once in the village, walking is easiest. Cobblestone streets and narrow lanes limit car access, adding to the charm.

Insider Experience Notes

- Many smaller stations are quiet and may have limited amenities. Bring snacks and water for rural journeys.
- Talk to locals; small coastal villages often have hidden viewpoints, private gardens, or local art galleries not widely advertised.
- Travel midweek or early morning to avoid peak summer crowds. This is particularly true for popular walking routes like the Seven Sisters or Jurassic Coast Path.
- Combine coastal and inland experiences. For example, a morning in Alfriston's South Downs followed by a gentle afternoon at Seaford beach offers a mix of hills and shoreline.

The South Coast is a treasure trove of hidden villages, tranquil beaches, and dramatic cliffs—all accessible by Britain's rail network. By blending train travel with local buses, short walks, and careful seasonal planning, travelers can escape the crowds and discover authentic coastal life. From the fishing harbor of Beer to the chalk cliffs of East Sussex, every stop offers history, culture, and natural beauty. Embrace the pace of the train, follow scenic paths, and sample local flavors to make each journey along Britain's southern coastline a memorable adventure.

CHAPTER 3
THE COTSWOLDS & OXFORD: IDYLLIC COUNTRYSIDE BY RAIL

The Cotswolds and Oxford offer a perfect escape from the bustling cities of Britain. The Cotswolds, with its rolling hills, charming villages, and idyllic landscapes, provides a taste of quintessential English countryside life. Oxford, just a short journey away, offers history, culture, and world-renowned architecture. Both destinations are easily accessible by train, making them ideal for a relaxing and enriching rail journey through southern England.

In this guide, we'll explore how to experience the best of the Cotswolds and Oxford by rail, highlighting scenic routes, must-see locations, cultural gems, food, and seasonal tips.

The Cotswolds: A Journey Through Time and Nature

The Cotswolds is an area of outstanding natural beauty, offering visitors a peaceful retreat with its quaint villages, stone cottages, and undulating hills. While the region is easily explored by car, traveling by train offers a unique way to take in the scenery and enjoy the slower pace of life.

Cotswolds Tour from London

Getting to the Cotswolds by Train

The Cotswolds is well-connected to London and other major cities by the Great Western Railway, with a journey from London Paddington to Moreton-in-Marsh taking around 1 hour 30 minutes. From here, local buses and taxis are available to take you to nearby villages such as Stow-on-the-Wold, Bourton-on-the-Water, and Chipping Campden, or you can explore on foot. Trains are frequent and convenient, making it easy to visit the Cotswolds as part of a longer rail tour of Southern England.

Cotswolds Private Train

If you're coming from Oxford, a train to Moreton-in-Marsh will take just under an hour. Once you've arrived, you can take a local bus or hire a bike to explore the villages, or simply enjoy the charming atmosphere of the market towns.

HIGHLIGHTS OF THE COTSWOLDS BY RAIL

The Cotswolds is best experienced by exploring its picture-perfect villages, ancient churches, and rolling landscapes. Some key spots to include on your journey are:

- **Bourton-on-the-Water**: Known as the "Venice of the Cotswolds," Bourton-on-the-Water is a must-see. The village is centered around the River Windrush, which winds through the town, lined with stone bridges and weeping willows. While here, enjoy a walk along the river or visit the Model Village, a 1:9 scale replica of the town itself.

- **Stow-on-the-Wold**: A historic market town, Stow-on-the-Wold is famous for its cobbled streets and honey-colored stone buildings. This charming village is also home to a wide variety of shops, antique stores, and traditional tearooms. The town square is a great place to stop for a coffee and soak in the atmosphere.
- **Chipping Campden**: A quintessential Cotswold town, Chipping Campden is known for its elegant High Street lined with historic buildings, including the 17th-century Market Hall. The town also serves as the starting point for the Cotswold Way, a long-distance walking trail that runs through the heart of the Cotswolds.
- **Broadway**: Another picturesque village, Broadway is often referred to as the "Jewel of the Cotswolds." Its wide main street is lined with attractive stone buildings, and there are plenty of pubs and restaurants where you can enjoy traditional English fare. Broadway Tower, located just outside the village, offers panoramic views of the surrounding countryside.

Things to Do in the Cotswolds

Beyond exploring the villages, the Cotswolds offers plenty of outdoor activities, including hiking, cycling, and horse riding. For those interested in history, the region is home to a number of historic sites, such as the 12th-century abbey in Tewkesbury and the medieval Sudeley Castle.

The Cotswold Way offers stunning walking routes with views across the countryside, and several local tour companies offer guided walks or cycle hire to make the most of the area's rural charm.

For food lovers, the Cotswolds offers a bounty of locally-sourced produce, including cheeses, meats, and seasonal vegetables. Enjoy a traditional pub lunch in one of the many village inns or visit a farmers' market to pick up fresh ingredients for a picnic.

Oxford: The City of Dreaming Spires

Just a short journey from the Cotswolds lies Oxford, the "City of Dreaming Spires." Famous for its university, which has educated many notable figures, including authors, politicians, and scientists, Oxford is a city rich in history and culture. The city's magnificent architecture, world-class museums, and beautiful gardens make it a must-visit destination when exploring Southern England by rail.

GETTING TO OXFORD BY TRAIN

Oxford is easily accessible from London by train. The journey from London Paddington to Oxford takes around 1 hour, with regular services throughout the day. If you're coming from the Cotswolds, a train from Moreton-in-Marsh to Oxford takes about 50 minutes. Upon arrival, the city is best explored on foot, as many of the major attractions are within walking distance of the train station.

Getting from London to Oxford - Footprints Tours

Highlights of Oxford by Rail

Oxford's historic colleges and their stunning architecture are the city's main draw, but there's much more to see and do beyond the university walls.

- **Oxford University**: The university is made up of 38 colleges, each with its own distinct character. Visit the Bodleian Library, one of the oldest libraries in Europe, or tour Christ Church College, famous for its connections to "Harry Potter" and its beautiful dining hall.

- **Radcliffe Camera and the Sheldonian Theatre**: Two of Oxford's most iconic buildings, the Radcliffe Camera and the Sheldonian Theatre, are located at the heart of the city. The Radcliffe Camera is an architectural masterpiece and houses part of the Bodleian Library, while the Sheldonian Theatre, designed by Sir Christopher Wren, is used for university ceremonies.
- **Parks and Gardens**: Oxford is home to a number of beautiful parks and gardens, including the University of Oxford Botanic Garden, which is the oldest botanic garden in Britain. Take a leisurely walk through the peaceful meadows of University Parks or visit the lovely Christchurch Meadow, where you can enjoy views of the River Thames and the spires of the city's colleges.
- **The Ashmolean Museum**: One of Oxford's most famous museums, the Ashmolean houses an impressive collection of art, archaeology, and history, including works by Leonardo da Vinci, ancient Egyptian artifacts, and European paintings from the Renaissance period.

Things to Do in Oxford

While Oxford is renowned for its academic history, there is also plenty of modern culture to enjoy. The city has a lively arts scene, with numerous galleries, theaters, and live music venues. If you're a fan of literature, visit The Eagle and Child pub, where J.R.R. Tolkien and C.S. Lewis used to meet with their literary group, the Inklings.

For a more relaxed day, take a punt along the River Thames, a quintessential Oxford experience. You can rent a punt and row yourself, or hire a punter to guide you along the river for a leisurely tour of the city's waterways.

Food and Drink in Oxford and the Cotswolds

The Cotswolds is known for its traditional British fare, with many villages offering cozy pubs and tearooms serving hearty dishes like steak and ale pie, ploughman's lunches, and freshly baked scones with clotted cream. In Oxford, you'll find a wide range of dining options, from casual cafes to upscale restaurants. For a true taste of Oxford, head to the Covered Market, where you'll find artisanal food stalls selling everything from local cheeses to freshly baked bread.

When to Visit the Cotswolds and Oxford

The Cotswolds and Oxford are great destinations year-round, but the best times to visit are in spring (April to June) and autumn (September to November). During these seasons, the countryside is at its most vibrant, with wildflowers in bloom and the autumn leaves turning golden. Summer can be busy, particularly in Oxford and the more tourist-heavy parts of the Cotswolds, while winter offers a peaceful, quieter experience, especially if you're looking for cozy pub lunches and winter walks.

The Cotswolds and Oxford offer a perfect blend of nature, history, and culture, all easily accessible by rail. Whether you're exploring the charming villages of the Cotswolds or soaking in the history of Oxford, both destinations offer an enriching experience that captures the heart of England. With convenient train connections, local buses, and plenty to see and do, your countryside adventure is just a train ride away.

SCENIC JOURNEYS THROUGH PICTURESQUE VILLAGES

Traveling by train across Britain allows travelers to explore not just major cities but also the **charming, often overlooked villages** that define the country's character. From the Cotswolds in central England to the rolling hills of Cornwall and the Scottish Highlands, rail journeys provide access to these hidden gems with comfort, ease, and scenic pleasure. This section highlights notable routes, practical tips, cultural insights, and seasonal recommendations, helping you plan a village-hopping adventure by train.

Fairy Tale-Like Villages in Europe

Choosing the Routes

Britain's network of main and branch lines makes picturesque villages surprisingly accessible. Some of the most scenic railways connecting villages include:

- **Cotswold Line (Oxford ↔ Worcester):** A gentle ride through limestone hills, historic market towns, and charming villages such as Chipping Campden, Moreton-in-Marsh, and Broadway (a short bus from the station).

- **Settle–Carlisle Line (Yorkshire ↔ Cumbria):** Known for dramatic viaducts and rolling hills, villages like Ribblehead and Giggleswick are perfect stops for a country walk or pub lunch.

- **West Highland Line (Glasgow ↔ Mallaig):** Remote Highland villages such as Arisaig and Lochailort showcase dramatic lochs, mountains, and coastlines.

- **Cambrian Coast Line (Shrewsbury ↔ Pwllheli):** Coastal villages like Barmouth, Aberdovey, and Harlech are accessible by rail with spectacular sea views.

- **Cornish Branch Lines (Penzance ↔ St Ives):** Quaint fishing villages such as St Just and Mousehole can be reached with short bus or walking connections.

Tip: Many of these routes are lightly serviced outside peak season. Always check the timetable in advance, especially for single-track sections.

Practical Travel Tips for Village Exploration

- **Station Proximity:** Some villages are a short walk from the station, while others require a local bus or taxi. For example, Broadway in the Cotswolds is 2 miles from the station, easily reached via local bus.

- **Off-Peak Travel:** For quieter trains and better value, travel off-peak or midweek. Summer weekends are popular, especially in tourist-friendly villages.

- **Tickets & Railcards:** National Rail offers advance, off-peak, and regional tickets. Railcards provide discounts for youths, seniors, or families.

- **Luggage:** Travel light; many village stations have no staffed services or luggage facilities. A small backpack makes local walks easier.

COTSWOLDS VILLAGES: HONEY-COLOURED STONE & MARKET TOWNS

Chipping Campden: Famous for its historic High Street and traditional crafts, this village is a 20-minute walk from Chipping Campden station. Explore artisan shops and the beautiful St James' Church.

Chipping Campden of beautiful St James' Church.

Moreton-in-Marsh: The station opens directly onto the town, making access simple. Visit the Tuesday market for local produce and antiques. Afternoon tea at **The Bell Inn** is highly recommended.

Broadway: A short bus from the station leads to this village, known for its Georgian and Tudor architecture. Broadway Tower, perched above the village, provides panoramic views of the surrounding countryside.

Seasonal Insight: Spring and summer offer vibrant gardens and walking trails. Autumn adds rich golden hues to the honey-colored stone villages, perfect for photography.

Yorkshire & Cumbria: Remote Villages Amid Stunning Landscapes

Ribblehead: Accessible from the Settle–Carlisle Line, Ribblehead is famous for the nearby **Ribblehead Viaduct**. Walks through moorland and valleys provide opportunities to spot sheep and local wildlife.

Giggleswick: A quaint village just a 10-minute walk from the station. Small cafes like **The Giggleswick Coffee House** serve local pastries and light lunches.

Appleby-in-Westmorland: Known for its medieval town center and the annual horse fair. The station is within walking distance, and the surrounding countryside is ideal for cycling or hiking.

Tip: In winter, the Settle–Carlisle line is quieter but offers snow-dusted landscapes, creating a postcard-worthy experience.

SCOTTISH HIGHLANDS: VILLAGES WITH DRAMATIC BACKDROPS

Arisaig & Lochailort: The West Highland Line connects Glasgow to these coastal villages. Small stations with minimal facilities lead to hiking trails, beaches, and traditional inns.

Mallaig: The terminus village is a fishing port, famous for fresh seafood. Walk to the harbor for local delicacies like scallops and smoked salmon. Ferry connections to the Isles of Skye and Small Isles are easily arranged.

Personal Insight: Sitting on a west-facing train seat from Fort William to Mallaig, watching lochs and mountains unfold, feels like a slow cinematic journey. Early morning or late afternoon light enhances the scenery.

Wales: Coastal & Mountain Villages

Barmouth & Aberdovey: On the Cambrian Coast Line, these villages offer sandy beaches and Victorian piers. Stations are a short walk from the center.

Harlech: A small village with a stunning castle on a hill. From Harlech Station, a 15-minute walk uphill takes you to the fortress, providing views over the sea and dunes.

Seasonal Tip: Summer is ideal for beach walks, while spring and autumn offer quieter trails for photography and birdwatching along the coast.

Wales Mountain Villages

Cornwall & South-West England: Fishing Villages & Coastal Charm

St Ives: From St Erth station (change from the main line at Penzance), a short branch line leads directly to this popular art town. Explore galleries, sandy beaches, and coastal walks.

Mousehole & St Just: Short bus rides from Penzance or other local stations take you to these small fishing villages with narrow lanes, traditional pubs, and artisan shops.

Food Insight: Cornish pasties, fresh seafood, and cream teas are highlights. Look for family-run bakeries and harbor-front cafes for authentic flavors.

On-Foot Exploration & Local Transfers

- **Walking:** Many village stations are within 10–20 minutes' walk of the center. Comfortable shoes are essential, as cobbled streets and uneven paths are common.
- **Buses & Taxis:** For villages a few miles from the station, local buses run less frequently in winter. Pre-booked taxis or ride-share apps may be necessary.

- **Cycling:** Some villages offer bike rentals, which is perfect for short countryside loops or coastal trails.

Tip: Ask at the station or local tourist offices for walking maps; these often include historical notes and recommended viewpoints.

Cultural & Seasonal Highlights

- **Festivals & Fairs:** Villages often host annual events, such as harvest festivals, Christmas markets, or local craft fairs. Checking local tourism websites helps time visits for these experiences.
- **Cuisine:** Village pubs and tea rooms often serve local specialties, from Cornish pasties to Welsh cakes. Seasonal menus highlight fresh, regional ingredients.
- **Photography:** Early morning or late afternoon provides the best light for capturing honey-colored cottages, riverside reflections, and rolling hills.

Personal Insight

Traveling through Britain's villages by train is a slower, more immersive experience than driving. The train offers a **window into changing landscapes**, while stepping off in each village allows interaction with locals, exploration of traditional pubs, and access to hidden historic gems. Some of my most memorable journeys include sipping tea in a Cotswold inn after a misty morning walk, or watching the sunset over a fishing harbor in Cornwall after a gentle train ride along the coast.

A key insight: **plan for flexibility**. Village trains can be infrequent, so allow extra time for walking, local buses, or exploring unexpected corners. This approach transforms a simple rail journey into a cultural and scenic adventure.

Britain's **picturesque villages are best experienced by train**, combining comfort, scenery, and accessibility. From the honey-colored cottages of the Cotswolds to the dramatic coasts of Scotland and Cornwall, each journey offers unique landscapes, cultural experiences, and seasonal delights. With careful planning, attention to local transfers, and an openness to explore on foot, travelers can enjoy authentic village life, historic architecture, local cuisine, and breathtaking views—all without the stress of driving or parking.

By incorporating scenic village stops into a rail itinerary, you experience **the heart of Britain**: quiet charm, rich heritage, and unspoiled countryside that stays long in the memory.

OXFORD: THE CITY OF DREAMING SPIRES

Oxford, known worldwide as the "City of Dreaming Spires," is a timeless destination that combines historic architecture, academic prestige, and vibrant culture. Traveling by train to Oxford is both convenient and scenic, offering views of rolling countryside and charming market towns along the way. This guide provides everything a rail traveler needs to explore Oxford efficiently, enjoy its cultural highlights, and discover hidden gems.

Oxford by Train region

Getting to Oxford by Train

Oxford is located roughly 60 miles northwest of London, making it an ideal day trip or overnight destination.

- **From London Paddington:** Trains operated by Great Western Railway depart frequently, with journey times of about 55–60 minutes. Most trains are modern and comfortable, with free Wi-Fi and onboard refreshments. Window seats on the left offer a pleasant view of the Thames Valley as you leave London.

- **From London Marylebone or Birmingham:** Chiltern Railways runs services from Marylebone via High Wycombe. From Birmingham, direct trains via Chiltern Railways take roughly 90 minutes.
- **Regional Connections:** Oxford also connects to Didcot Parkway, Reading, and Banbury, providing flexibility for travelers exploring southern England or the Cotswolds.

Practical Tip: Advance booking is recommended for morning trains, especially during university term or tourist peak season.

OXFORD STATION TO THE CITY CENTER

Oxford Railway Station is located about 1 mile southeast of the city center.

- **By Bus:** Stagecoach buses (routes 1 and 2) run every 10–15 minutes to central stops near the High Street and Carfax Tower. Travel time is roughly 10 minutes.
- **On Foot:** A pleasant 20-minute walk follows Botley Road and Magdalen Street, with cafés, shops, and bookshops en route.
- **By Taxi or Rideshare:** A 5-minute drive for convenience or if carrying luggage.

Insider Tip: Walking offers a gentle introduction to Oxford's architecture, from Victorian terraces to modern university buildings, and helps orient you before exploring the historic heart.

Historic Highlights and University Colleges

Oxford is synonymous with its university, and exploring the colleges is central to the experience:

- **Christ Church College:** Famous for its cathedral, grand dining hall, and filming connections to Harry Potter. The meadows behind the college provide peaceful walks along the River Thames.
- **Magdalen College:** Offers a beautiful deer park, ancient cloisters, and a riverside walk along the Cherwell.

- **Radcliffe Camera and Bodleian Library:** Architectural masterpieces in the city center. Guided tours of the Bodleian reveal medieval reading rooms and historic manuscripts.

Practical Tip: Many colleges charge a small entry fee. Visiting early in the morning avoids crowds and allows photography without obstruction.

Museums and Cultural Experiences

Oxford's museums make excellent stops for both cultural and family travelers:

- **Ashmolean Museum:** Britain's first public museum, with collections spanning Egyptian antiquities to modern art. Entry is free, and temporary exhibitions are worth checking online.

- **Pitt Rivers Museum:** Adjacent to the Oxford University Museum of Natural History, this museum displays anthropological artifacts in densely packed cases—a unique visual experience.

- **Museum of the History of Science:** Offers insight into early scientific instruments and inventions, appealing to those interested in innovation and history.

Personal Insight: I've found the combination of the Ashmolean's classic galleries and the Pitt Rivers' curious artifacts makes for a full morning of indoor exploration, particularly useful on rainy days.

WALKING THE CITY AND PUNTING ON THE RIVERS

Oxford's compact size makes it ideal for exploring on foot:

- **High Street and Cornmarket Street:** Lined with historic shops, bookshops, and cafés. Look for traditional sweet shops and local produce stores.

- **University Parks and Botanic Garden:** Gentle walks and seasonal flowers provide a peaceful escape from the busier streets.

- **Punting on the Cherwell or Thames:** Hire a punt from Magdalen Bridge Boathouse or Cherwell Boathouse. You can choose to hire a chauffeured punt or try steering yourself. Summer afternoons offer scenic views of college gardens and weeping willows.

Travel Insight: Renting a punt in spring or summer gives a calm perspective of Oxford's rivers and bridges. Off-season, shorter walks along the rivers still provide excellent scenery.

Food and Dining Options

Oxford combines traditional English fare with international cuisine:

- **Traditional Pubs:** The Eagle and Child, historic haunt of the Inklings writers, serves hearty classics such as pies and fish and chips.
- **Cafés and Tearooms:** Turl Street Kitchen and Vaults & Garden Café offer local pastries, sandwiches, and coffee in charming historic settings.
- **Fine Dining:** Quod Restaurant or The Cherwell Boathouse offer modern British cuisine with riverside views, ideal for lunch or dinner.

Practical Tip: For a quick, affordable lunch, pick up items from the Covered Market—local cheeses, meats, and baked goods make excellent picnic options for exploring the parks or riverside.

Seasonal Highlights

Oxford changes character with the seasons, enhancing the travel experience:

- **Spring (March–May):** College gardens bloom, riversides are vibrant, and the weather is mild for walking.
- **Summer (June–August):** Punting and outdoor dining are at their peak; guided walking tours and events are frequent.
- **Autumn (September–November):** Golden leaves in University Parks and along riverbanks create picturesque scenes. Less crowded than summer, ideal for photography.
- **Winter (December–February):** Crisp air, festive lights, and cozy pubs make city exploration atmospheric. Museums provide a warm refuge during shorter days.

Personal Tip: Early morning walks in autumn highlight the city's "dreaming spires" before tourists arrive, creating memorable photographs and a serene experience.

Shopping and Hidden Gems

Oxford offers more than its famous university:

- **Covered Market:** Traditional stalls with artisanal products, cheeses, baked goods, and gifts. A great place to pick up souvenirs.
- **Blackwell's Bookshop:** Legendary for rare books and academic texts; the Norrington Room has over 160,000 titles in a single space.
- **Hidden Walkways:** St Giles' and the back alleys near Radcliffe Square offer quiet spots away from main streets, often overlooked by tourists.

Insider Tip: Explore off the beaten path for local cafés and small galleries; they often showcase contemporary art and crafts inspired by Oxford's historic environment.

Day Trips from Oxford

Oxford is a perfect base for scenic or cultural excursions by rail:

- **Blenheim Palace (Woodstock):** 15-minute bus or taxi from Oxford station. Magnificent estate with gardens and exhibitions, birthplace of Winston Churchill.
- **Cotswolds Villages:** Trains to Moreton-in-Marsh (via Worcester or Banbury) open access to honey-colored villages, countryside walks, and historic pubs.
- **Stratford-upon-Avon:** About 1.5 hours by train; Shakespeare's birthplace offers theaters, riverside walks, and period architecture.

Travel Insight: Combining a half-day in Oxford with an afternoon trip to Blenheim Palace provides a mix of city charm and grand country estate scenery.

PRACTICAL MAP FOR RAIL TRAVELERS

- **Step 1:** Train from London Paddington → Oxford (55–60 min).
- **Step 2:** Bus, walk, or taxi → Oxford city center, near High Street/Cornmarket.
- **Step 3:** Explore historic colleges, museums, and parks on foot. Optional punting on Cherwell/Thames.
- **Step 4:** Lunch or afternoon tea at local cafés or pubs; stop at Covered Market for snacks or souvenirs.
- **Step 5:** Optional short trip to Blenheim Palace, Cotswolds, or Stratford-upon-Avon via bus/train.

- **Step 6:** Return to Oxford station for onward travel.

This sequence provides flexibility, balance between sightseeing and relaxation, and clear directional guidance for first-time visitors.

Oxford by train is a travel experience that blends culture, history, and the beauty of the English countryside. The rail journey itself is scenic, and arriving by train places you in the heart of a city designed for walking. From exploring medieval colleges to punting along the river, Oxford combines academic prestige, local charm, and culinary delights. Planning your visit with time for museums, gardens, and hidden streets ensures a complete and memorable experience—truly living up to its nickname, the "City of Dreaming Spires."

A SLOW TRAVEL DAY IN THE HEART OF THE COTSWOLDS

The Cotswolds, with its honey-colored stone villages, lush valleys, and historic market towns, is one of Britain's most picturesque regions. Traveling here by train allows you to experience its charm at a relaxed pace, blending scenic rail journeys with gentle walks, local culture, and culinary delights. A "slow travel" day in the Cotswolds emphasizes exploration over speed, letting you savor the region's beauty, history, and food without rush.

Slow Travel in the Cotswolds

GETTING THERE BY TRAIN

Rail Routes

The Cotswolds are well connected by train, though many villages require a short local transfer. Key stations include:

- **Moreton-in-Marsh (GWR, London Paddington – 1 hour 45 minutes)**: A hub for exploring northern Cotswolds villages.
- **Kingham (GWR, London Paddington – 1 hour 40 minutes)**: Convenient for southern villages like Stow-on-the-Wold and Chipping Norton.
- **Stroud (GWR, London Paddington – 2 hours)**: Ideal for the western edge of the Cotswolds and the Stroud Valleys.

Transfers

- Taxis and local buses connect stations to surrounding villages. For example, from Moreton-in-Marsh, a 5-minute taxi ride reaches Bourton-on-the-Water, while local buses can take you to Stow-on-the-Wold and Lower Slaughter.
- Some villages, like Bibury or Upper Slaughter, are best reached on foot from nearby stations or as part of a walking itinerary.

Morning: A Gentle Start in Moreton-in-Marsh

Station and Village

Arrive at Moreton-in-Marsh early to enjoy the calm before the day-trippers arrive. The station itself is small and welcoming, with a café for coffee and pastries.

- Walk 5–10 minutes into the village to explore the market square. The 17th-century market hall is still in use for local crafts, antiques, and fresh produce.
- Stroll along High Street to admire classic Cotswold stone cottages, artisan shops, and cozy bookshops.

Local Breakfast

- Stop at a local tearoom such as **Café T** or **The Gourmet Café** for traditional English breakfast or freshly baked pastries.
- Seasonal insight: In spring, enjoy fresh strawberries or rhubarb from local farms. In autumn, warm apple tarts and cider are excellent.

Late Morning: Scenic Village Walks

Bourton-on-the-Water

- **Access:** 5-minute taxi or 30-minute walk along country lanes from Moreton-in-Marsh.
- Often called the "Venice of the Cotswolds," Bourton-on-the-Water is famous for its low stone bridges spanning the River Windrush.
- Explore the village at leisure: the model village, quaint cafes, and riverside paths are perfect for slow exploration.

Walking Insight

- Walking along the river offers a peaceful contrast to the busier streets. Stop on benches or grassy banks to watch ducks and local anglers.
- The village is compact; you can cover the main streets and riverside in under 90 minutes, leaving time for a relaxed coffee at a riverside café.

Lunch: Seasonal Flavors and Local Cuisine

- For a quintessential Cotswolds experience, choose a village pub such as **The Bell at Bourton** or **The Old Manse Hotel** in nearby Stow-on-the-Wold.
- Recommended dishes: locally sourced lamb, seasonal vegetables, and freshly baked bread. Many pubs also offer artisan cheeses from nearby farms.
- Pair your meal with a local ale or cider. For those traveling slowly, take time to sit outside if weather permits—autumn light over stone cottages is unforgettable.

AFTERNOON: VILLAGE HOPPING BY TRAIN AND FOOT

Stow-on-the-Wold

- **Access:** Bus or taxi from Bourton-on-the-Water (10–15 minutes).
- Highlights: Market Square with antique shops, historic churches like St. Edward's, and the classic Cotswold architecture lining the streets.
- Personal Insight: Arrive mid-afternoon for a quieter experience; many day visitors depart by this time, allowing for leisurely exploration and photography without crowds.

Lower Slaughter

- **Access:** 2-mile walk from Stow-on-the-Wold through gentle country lanes, about 40 minutes.
- This small village is a picture-perfect spot with a single main street and river, traditional stone cottages, and a historic water mill.
- Walking Tips: Bring comfortable shoes; paths are well-maintained but can be uneven near the river. Spring wildflowers and autumn leaves enhance the charm.

Optional Stop: Upper Slaughter

- Continue walking from Lower Slaughter (20 minutes) to Upper Slaughter for a serene countryside experience. Fewer tourists make this ideal for reflective strolls and photography.
- Seasonal tip: Winter mornings can be misty, creating magical views of the stone cottages and countryside.

Afternoon Tea and Local Treats

- Pause at a village tea shop for Cotswold cream tea—scones with clotted cream and jam—paired with locally blended tea.
- Personal Insight: Village tea shops often feature homemade cakes with ingredients sourced from nearby farms, adding an authentic taste of the region.

Evening: Return by Train

- **Stations for Departure:** Return to Moreton-in-Marsh or Kingham for trains back to London or onward destinations.
- Recommended: Aim for the late afternoon or early evening train to enjoy sunset views over rolling fields and distant hills from the carriage window.

Onboard Experience

- Sit on the right-hand side for views of the Windrush Valley. Rolling hills, grazing sheep, and scattered farmhouses create a quintessential Cotswold landscape.
- Bring a notebook or camera: the slow pace of the train allows time to notice details often missed when driving.

Cultural Highlights Along the Route

- Many villages feature historic churches, manor houses, and small museums. For example:
    - **Bourton-on-the-Water Model Village**: Miniature replicas of village landmarks.
    - **Stow Market Hall**: Antique and craft stalls reflecting local artisanship.
    - **Slaughter villages**: Traditional water mills and historic cottages, some dating back to the 1600s.
- Seasonal festivals:
    - Spring: Cotswold Show Gardens and flower festivals in various villages.
    - Autumn: Harvest festivals and local cider tastings.

Slow Travel Tips

- Embrace walking: The best way to experience the villages is on foot. The distances are short, and walking lets you absorb architecture, local life, and landscape.
- Use local taxis and buses for short transfers, avoiding long waits or driving.
- Avoid peak weekend times if you prefer quiet. Weekdays are ideal for slow, reflective exploration.
- Pack light: Daypacks with water, snacks, camera, and layered clothing are sufficient.
- Keep an eye on weather: Cotswold mornings can be misty, afternoons sunny, and evenings chilly, even in summer.

A slow travel day in the Cotswolds combines scenic train rides, gentle walks, historic villages, and local cuisine. Start at Moreton-in-Marsh, explore Bourton-on-the-Water and Stow-on-the-Wold, then wander through Lower and Upper Slaughter. Take time for coffee, afternoon tea, or a pub lunch. Use local transfers efficiently and enjoy the landscapes from both train and foot. The result is a day of unhurried exploration, connecting with nature, history, and culture in one of England's most idyllic regions.

CHAPTER 4
NORTHERN ENGLAND: PEAKS, PUBS & LAKES

Northern England is a region that blends rugged landscapes, historic towns, and a culture steeped in tradition. From the towering peaks of the Lake District to the gentle hills of the Peak District, this part of Britain offers a wealth of natural beauty and rich heritage, all easily accessible by train. Whether you're hiking through the fells, exploring ancient castles, or relaxing in cozy village pubs, Northern England promises an unforgettable rail journey through its picturesque countryside.

This section will guide you through the must-see destinations in Northern England, focusing on the best train routes, top attractions, local experiences, food, and seasonal tips.

Northern England train travel route

GETTING TO NORTHERN ENGLAND BY TRAIN

Northern England is well-connected to major cities like London, Manchester, and Liverpool, making it easy to access by rail. Train services are frequent, with several routes offering scenic views of the countryside along the way.

- **From London to the Lake District**: You can catch a direct train from London Euston to Oxenholme (Lake District) in about 3 hours. From Oxenholme, local trains can take you to popular spots like Windermere, Kendal, and Ambleside. For a more scenic experience, consider taking the West Coast Main Line or the Lakes Line, both of which offer picturesque views of the surrounding countryside.

From London to the Lake District train routes

- **From Manchester to the Peak District**: Trains from Manchester Piccadilly to Edale (the gateway to the Peak District) takes just 45 minutes, offering quick access to one of the most popular national parks in Britain. From Edale, you can easily explore the area on foot or by bus.
- **From Liverpool to the Lake District**: Trains from Liverpool Lime Street to the Lake District typically take around 2.5 hours, with direct routes to stations like Windermere and Barrow-in-Furness, connecting visitors to the heart of the region.

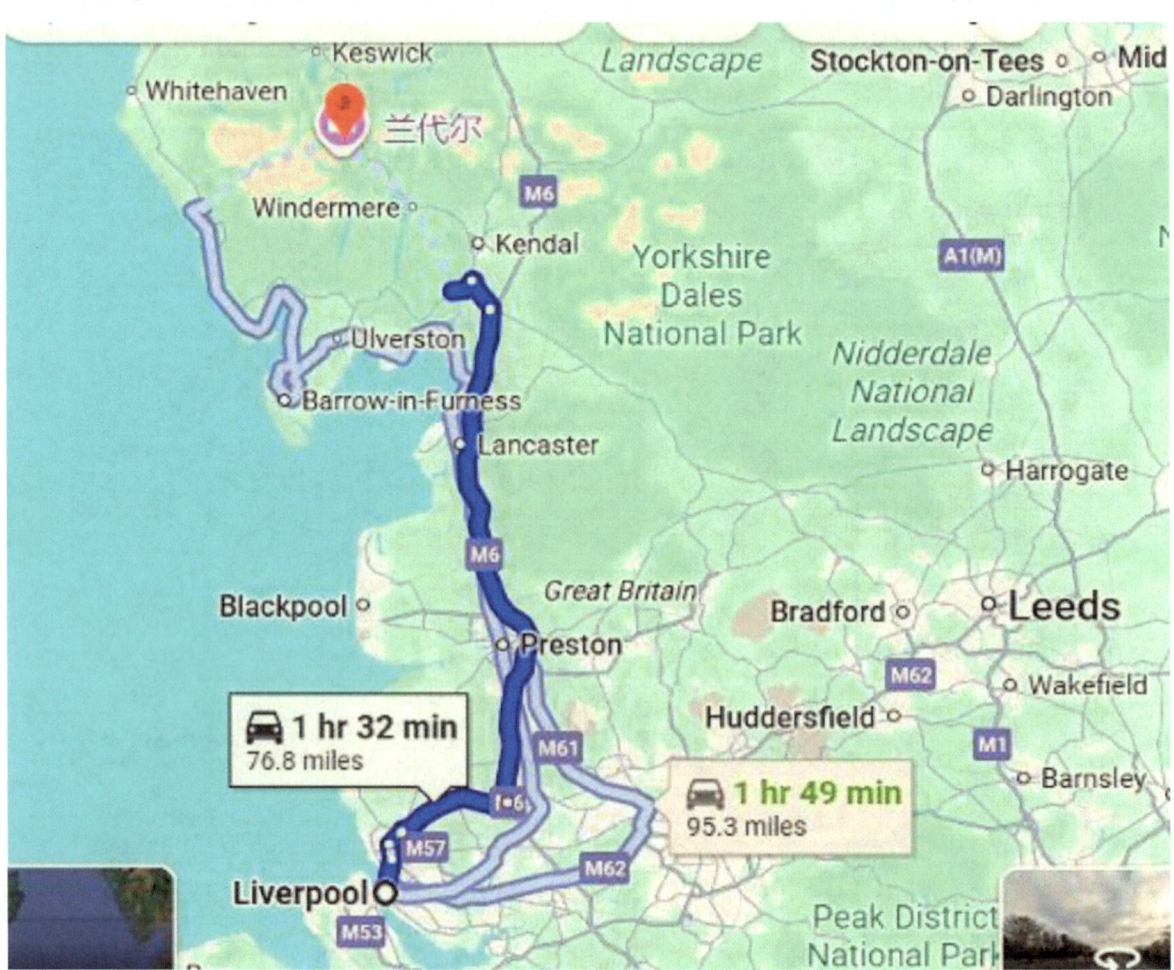

From Liverpool to the Lake District atlas

Highlights of Northern England: Lakes, Peaks & History

The Lake District: Natural Beauty and Tranquil Waters

The Lake District, a UNESCO World Heritage site, is the crown jewel of Northern England's landscapes. Known for its crystal-clear lakes, rolling hills, and charming villages, it is a haven for nature lovers and outdoor enthusiasts. The Lake District is perfect for hikers, cyclists, and those seeking peace and solitude in nature.

- **Windermere**: The largest lake in England, Windermere is the perfect base for exploring the Lake District. You can catch a train from Oxenholme to Windermere in about 20 minutes. Once in Windermere, explore the lake by boat, enjoy scenic walks, or visit the nearby village of Bowness-on-Windermere. The area is also known for Beatrix Potter's former home, Hill Top, which is a must-visit for fans of Peter Rabbit.

- **Keswick and Derwentwater**: Situated on the shores of Derwentwater, Keswick is a vibrant market town offering easy access to some of the best hiking in the region. Take a boat ride on the lake or explore the many trails around the surrounding fells, including the popular walk up to Catbells, which offers panoramic views of the lake and the surrounding mountains.

- **Grasmere**: A picturesque village nestled in the heart of the Lake District; Grasmere is famous for its association with poet William Wordsworth. Visit his former home, Dove Cottage, and stroll through the village to sample the famous Grasmere gingerbread, a local delicacy.

THE PEAK DISTRICT: MAJESTIC HILLS AND QUAINT VILLAGES

Just a short train ride from Manchester, the Peak District National Park is known for its dramatic landscapes, including limestone hills, deep valleys, and picturesque villages. The region offers a diverse range of outdoor activities, from hiking and cycling to caving and rock climbing.

- **Edale**: The starting point of the famous Pennine Way, Edale is a small village in the heart of the Peak District. From here, you can hike up to the top of Kinder Scout, the highest point in the park, or explore the beautiful valley of Hope. The village itself is charming, with several pubs serving traditional ales and hearty meals.

- **Bakewell**: Known for its delicious Bakewell tart, this historic market town sits on the River Wye. Take a stroll along the river or visit the famous Bakewell Farmers' Market for local produce. The nearby Chatsworth House, one of England's finest stately homes, is a must-see, offering beautiful gardens and historic interiors.
- **Castleton**: A small village set within a limestone gorge, Castleton is a great base for exploring the caves and hills of the Peak District. Visit the Blue John Cavern to see the rare Blue John stone, or take a hike up to the ruins of Peveril Castle, which offers breathtaking views of the surrounding area.

Local Culture and Food: Traditional Pubs and Regional Delights

One of the highlights of Northern England is the region's vibrant pub culture. After a day of hiking, cycling, or sightseeing, there's nothing better than unwinding in a cozy local pub with a pint of local ale and some hearty food.

- **Lake District Pubs**: Many of the pubs in the Lake District have a long history, serving travelers for centuries. The *Drunken Duck Inn* near Ambleside is a local favorite, offering great food, local ales, and stunning views of the surrounding fells. Similarly, the *The King's Arms* in Hawkshead is a historic pub with an inviting atmosphere and a menu full of traditional Cumbrian dishes.
- **Peak District Pubs**: In the Peak District, pubs like the *Old Hall Hotel* in Hope Valley and the *The Royal Oak* in Bakewell serve classic pub fare, including hearty pies, lamb, and local cheeses. The Peak District is also home to several traditional breweries, including *Peak District Brewing Company*, offering a variety of ales to sample.
- **Regional Specialties**: Northern England is known for its rich, comforting cuisine. In the Lake District, try *Cumberland sausage*, a flavorful, coiled sausage made from pork and seasoned with herbs and spices. In the Peak District, *Bakewell tart* is a must-try dessert, with a short crust base, jam, and almond-flavored sponge.

Seasonal Tips for Northern England

Northern England offers something for every season, with each time of year bringing its own unique charm. The best time to visit depends on the kind of experience you're after.

- **Spring and Summer**: These seasons bring warmer weather and longer days, perfect for hiking and outdoor activities. The Lake District's wildflowers are in bloom, and the Peak District is lush and green. However, these seasons also attract the most visitors, so popular spots like Windermere and Keswick can get crowded. Early mornings or weekdays are the best times to visit for a quieter experience.

- **Autumn**: Autumn is a fantastic time to visit Northern England, with the landscapes turning golden and red. The weather is still mild, and the crowds have thinned. It's a great time to explore the countryside on foot or by bike, and to visit the local pubs for a warming meal and a pint of local ale.
- **Winter**: While the winter months are quieter, Northern England can be quite magical at this time of year. The snow-capped peaks of the Lake District and Peak District create a picturesque winter wonderland. If you're visiting during the colder months, pack appropriately for the weather and check for any disruptions to travel due to snow or ice.

Northern England offers a wealth of experiences that are best explored by rail. From the tranquil lakes of the Lake District to the rugged peaks of the Peak District, the region provides a perfect combination of outdoor adventure, historical sites, and cozy village life. Whether you're a hiker, history buff, or simply seeking a peaceful retreat, Northern England promises a journey filled with natural beauty, rich culture, and unforgettable memories.

With easy access by train from major cities and a range of local transport options, exploring the region by rail is both practical and scenic, making it the ideal way to experience the best that this stunning part of Britain has to offer.

THE LAKE DISTRICT: HIKING & LAKESIDE VIEWS FROM THE TRAIN

The **Lake District** in northwest England is one of Britain's most scenic regions, famous for its glacial lakes, rugged fells, and quaint villages. Traveling by train offers a stress-free, scenic way to access this UNESCO World Heritage area, linking major towns, rural stations, and trailheads with minimal need for a car. From rolling lakeside paths to dramatic hiking trails, the train is both a comfortable and environmentally friendly way to explore.

The Lake District in northwest England Atlas

KEY TRAIN ROUTES TO THE LAKE DISTRICT

The Lake District is served primarily by **Northern Rail** and **Avanti West Coast**, with main hubs at **Oxenholme Lake District**, **Windermere**, and **Penrith**. These stations provide convenient access to hiking trails, lakes, and villages.

- **London to Oxenholme Lake District:** Direct services from **London Euston** via Avanti West Coast take approximately **2 hours 40 minutes**. Oxenholme is a central gateway, with onward connections to Windermere or local villages.

- **Manchester to Windermere:** Northern Rail offers frequent services via **Lancaster**, taking around **1 hour 30 minutes**. Ideal for day trips from Manchester.

- **Carlisle to Windermere:** Scenic regional trains pass through Eden Valley and the northern fells, connecting towns such as **Kendal** and **Staveley**.

Transfers & Local Access:

- From Oxenholme, take a **15–20-minute Northern Rail train to Windermere**, the Lake District's main tourist town.
- Local buses, taxis, and even seasonal water taxis connect lakeside villages such as **Ambleside, Bowness-on-Windermere**, and **Grasmere**.

Practical Tip: Book seats on the left-hand side of southbound trains from Oxenholme to Windermere for uninterrupted lake views.

Windermere: Lakeside Base and Village Charm

Windermere Station is within walking distance of the town center and the shores of **Lake Windermere**, England's largest lake. This town is the ideal base for hiking, boating, and cultural exploration.

the Charm of the Prettiest Lake District

Lakeside Activities:

- **Boat Tours:** Steamers run along the lake to Ambleside, Bowness, and Lakeside. These provide a unique perspective of the fells and waterside villages.
- **Walking Paths:** Lakeside promenades are perfect for gentle walks, with cafes and viewpoints along the way. The **Orrest Head Trail** is a short, accessible climb offering panoramic views of Windermere and surrounding fells.

Food & Drink:

- **Homeground Coffee + Kitchen:** Artisan coffee and light meals, ideal for pre- or post-hike fuel.
- **The Crafty Baa:** Offers hearty local dishes, including Lakeland lamb and freshwater fish.

Seasonal Insight: Spring and summer provide the most reliable lake conditions and colorful wildflowers along trails, while autumn brings fiery foliage across the fells.

Ambleside & Grasmere: Village Exploration on Foot

Ambleside: A short bus or 20-minute walk from Windermere, Ambleside is a hub for hiking and culture. The **Stock Ghyll Force waterfall** walk begins directly from town. Ambleside has outdoor shops, traditional pubs, and craft stores.

Grasmere: Accessible by a 15–20-minute bus from Ambleside, Grasmere is famous for its historic connections to **William Wordsworth**. Visit **Dove Cottage** and sample the famous **Grasmere Gingerbread** from Sarah Nelson's shop.

Hiking Routes:

- Easy to moderate walks include **Loughrigg Fell** from Ambleside, offering lakeside views and panoramic summits within 2–3 hours.
- For a full-day hike, **Helm Crag and Easedale Tarn** provide moderate challenges with spectacular lake and valley vistas.

Personal Insight: Walking from Grasmere to Rydal Water early in the morning offers quiet trails and wildlife spotting, including red squirrels and herons, before tourist traffic builds.

CONISTON & HAWKSHEAD: NORTHERN LAKESIDE ADVENTURES

Coniston: Reachable via bus or taxi from Oxenholme or Windermere, Coniston Water is smaller but surrounded by dramatic fells. **The Old Man of Coniston** is a classic hike, providing challenging climbs and exceptional lake views.

Coniston coastal adventure

Hawkshead: Accessible by bus from Windermere or Ambleside, this village retains historic charm with cobbled streets and whitewashed cottages. **Beatrix Potter Gallery** is a cultural highlight.

Food & Drink:

- **Bluebird Café (Coniston):** Fresh Lake trout and traditional Lakeland dishes.
- **Queen's Head, Hawkshead:** Offers locally sourced menus in a cozy village pub atmosphere.

Seasonal Consideration: Summer is ideal for lake-side boating and longer hikes, while winter offers crisp, clear visibility of fells for photographers but requires warmer clothing and sturdy boots for muddy trails.

Scenic Rail Highlights

- **Oxenholme to Windermere:** Rolling hills, rivers, and glimpses of Lake Windermere itself.
- **Kendal to Windermere:** Pastureland dotted with farmsteads, wooded valleys, and historic stone bridges.
- **Coniston Bus Connections:** Lakeside roads bordered by fells, giving a sense of remoteness without long walks from the train.

Tip: Keep a camera or smartphone ready—many trains pass through open countryside with no barriers, offering uninterrupted panoramic views.

Hiking & Lakeside Experiences

- **Short Hikes:** Orrest Head, Stock Ghyll Force, and Grasmere to Rydal Water offer 1–3-hour walks, suitable for most travelers.
- **Full-Day Hikes:** Helvellyn, Catbells, and The Old Man of Coniston provide more challenging climbs with spectacular payoff. Bring water, snacks, and proper footwear.
- **Water-Based Adventures:** Kayaking, paddleboarding, or boat cruises on Windermere, Coniston, and Derwentwater give a different perspective of the fells.

Local Insight: Small village cafés often offer sandwiches, pastries, and packed lunches for hikers—supporting local businesses while fueling your exploration.

Cultural & Seasonal Highlights

- **Local Festivals:** Windermere hosts a summer music festival, while Grasmere hosts the **Rushbearing Festival** in late summer, celebrating village heritage with processions and music.
- **Cuisine:** Try Lakeland lamb, fresh trout, and Grasmere gingerbread. Many pubs source ingredients locally, enhancing authenticity.

- **Photography & Wildlife:** Dawn and dusk are ideal for photographing lakes and hills. Look for herons, swans, and red squirrels in quieter villages.

Personal Insight

Traveling the Lake District by train and connecting buses allows you to **experience the landscape slowly**—unlike driving, you can relax, watch the scenery, and plan walking routes without worrying about parking. My favorite route is from **Oxenholme to Windermere**, then walking along the lake to Ambleside, hopping a bus to Grasmere, and returning by late afternoon train—this gives a full variety of village charm, lakeside views, and easy hiking without needing a car.

Tip: Bring layers. The Lake District weather is famously unpredictable. Even in summer, a light waterproof jacket is invaluable.

The **Lake District by train** offers a combination of stunning lakeside views, accessible hiking, and charming village culture. Key hubs like Windermere, Ambleside, and Grasmere provide ideal bases for walking trails, boat excursions, and culinary experiences. Seasonal awareness enhances every trip: spring and summer for flowers and lake activities, autumn for vibrant foliage, and winter for crisp, atmospheric photography.

By using the train network, travelers can explore the heart of England's lake country efficiently, comfortably, and sustainably, while enjoying authentic village life, historic sites, and panoramic landscapes. This journey exemplifies why the Lake District remains one of Britain's most scenic and accessible natural destinations.

THE YORKSHIRE DALES: EXPLORING NATURE AND HERITAGE

The Yorkshire Dales, a region of rolling hills, limestone cliffs, and quaint villages, is one of Britain's most scenic destinations by train. Its combination of natural beauty, historic market towns, and rural charm makes it ideal for travelers seeking both outdoor adventure and cultural exploration. Traveling by rail allows you to enjoy the journey through picturesque valleys and rivers, while accessing hidden gems that are often missed by car. This guide provides a complete overview of routes, experiences, food, and practical travel tips for exploring the Yorkshire Dales.

The Yorkshire Dales waterfall

GETTING TO THE YORKSHIRE DALES BY TRAIN

Rail travel is the most scenic and relaxing way to reach the Dales:

- **From Leeds or York:** Northern Rail operates regular services to stations such as Skipton, Settle, and Harrogate, which serve as gateways to the Dales. Skipton, called the "Gateway to the Dales," is particularly well connected, with a journey of just over an hour from Leeds.

- **The Settle-Carlisle Line:** Considered one of the most beautiful railway journeys in Britain, this line runs through the heart of the Dales from Settle to Carlisle. Expect stunning viaducts, river valleys, and rolling hills along the way. The line is best experienced in daylight for optimal views.

- **From Manchester:** Direct trains to Skipton take around 1 hour 15 minutes. Changing at Leeds is also possible, offering a chance to glimpse Yorkshire's industrial heritage along the way.

Travel Insight: Always try to book a window seat on the left side traveling north from Leeds to see the Ribble Valley and limestone dales unfold.

Arriving in Skipton and Local Transfers

Skipton station is conveniently located near the town center, making onward exploration simple:

- **Walking:** A 5–10-minute walk takes you into the historic market town, past canal locks and cobbled streets.

- **Buses and Local Transfers:** DalesBus services connect Skipton to Malham, Grassington, Hawes, and other scenic spots in the heart of the Dales. These buses coordinate with train arrivals on weekends and in peak season.

- **Cycling:** Bike rentals are available near the station, ideal for exploring the surrounding valleys at your own pace.

Insider Tip: Skipton itself is worth half a day—its medieval castle, canal-sidewalks, and Saturday market provide a charming introduction to the Dales.

EXPLORING NATURAL LANDSCAPES

The Yorkshire Dales National Park offers dramatic scenery accessible by train and local transfers:

- **Malham Cove:** Take a bus or taxi from Skipton or Settle. This limestone amphitheater is iconic, with a flat walk from the village leading to dramatic cliffs. The Pennine Way and circular trails provide options for longer hikes.

- **Aysgarth Falls and Wensleydale:** Reachable from the Settle-Carlisle line via Garsdale or Hawes, the waterfalls are particularly impressive after rainfall. Trails along the river allow leisurely exploration and photography.

- **The Ribble Valley and Nidderdale:** Rolling hills and scenic rivers ideal for cycling or gentle walking. Local pubs along the way offer traditional fare and rest stops.

Travel Insight: Early morning walks in Malham or Aysgarth provide serene conditions and soft lighting for photography. During summer, weekdays are quieter, offering a more intimate experience of the landscape.

Heritage and Historic Villages

Beyond natural beauty, the Dales are rich in history and culture:

- **Hawes:** A market town famous for Wensleydale cheese. Stop at the Wensleydale Creamery to see cheese-making and enjoy tastings. Hawes also features narrow cobbled streets and local craft shops.
- **Grassington:** A picturesque village with stone cottages, boutique shops, and riverside walks. It hosts seasonal festivals such as the Grassington Festival in summer.
- **Settle:** Offers a historic town center, weekly markets, and access to the Settle-Carlisle railway for scenic rides. The Ribblehead Viaduct, just outside the town, is a must-see engineering marvel set against moorland hills.

Personal Insight: Spending a night in a village like Hawes or Grassington allows you to experience the Dales at dusk and dawn, when the light turns the hills golden and the towns feel almost timeless.

Food and Local Cuisine

The Yorkshire Dales are known for hearty, local fare and artisanal products:

- **Traditional Pubs:** Try local lamb dishes, Yorkshire pudding, and cask ales at historic inns such as The Golden Lion in Grassington or The George in Hawes.
- **Wensleydale Cheese:** Sample and purchase at the Wensleydale Creamery or local farm shops. Pair with oatcakes and local chutneys for a perfect picnic.
- **Cafés and Tearooms:** Skipton Market and Settle's cafés serve locally baked cakes, scones, and sandwiches ideal for packed lunches on scenic walks.

Travel Tip: Pack a picnic for longer hikes—it allows you to stop at viewpoints and enjoy the scenery without rushing back to towns.

Seasonal Highlights

Season affects both scenery and accessibility:

- **Spring (March–May):** Wildflowers bloom, rivers are full, and lambs graze in the fields. Ideal for walking and cycling.
- **Summer (June–August):** Longer daylight hours for exploration; bus services run more frequently, and festival season begins in villages.
- **Autumn (September–November):** Golden foliage and quieter trails. Mild weather is perfect for hiking.

- **Winter (December–February):** Snow-capped hills and crisp air create a dramatic landscape. Some rural bus services are limited; plan transfers carefully.

Insider Tip: Autumn light enhances the contrast of dry-stone walls, green valleys, and heather-topped hills, making photography particularly rewarding.

Scenic Train Journeys Within the Dales

Several rail routes offer breathtaking views:

- **Settle to Carlisle:** One of Britain's most iconic lines, passing through Ribblehead Viaduct, Dent, and Appleby. Stop at stations along the way for walks or village exploration.

- **Skipton to Carlisle (via Settle):** Offers a combination of moorland, limestone cliffs, and rivers. Tickets can be purchased in advance, and first-class seating provides panoramic windows.

- **Leeds to Morecambe (Coastal Extension):** For those extending the trip, trains pass through the western edges of the Dales before reaching the Lancashire coast.

Travel Insight: Keep a camera handy for views of viaducts and distant hills; try to sit on the left side northbound for the most dramatic vistas.

Walking and Outdoor Activities

Walking is central to experiencing the Yorkshire Dales:

- **Short Walks:** Malham Tarn, Janet's Foss waterfall, and the village trails in Grassington are ideal for casual exploration.

- **Longer Hikes:** Pennine Way sections, Ingleborough routes, and circular hikes from Settle or Hawes provide immersive experiences for serious walkers.

- **Cycling:** Quiet lanes connect Skipton, Grassington, and Malham. Bike rentals are available in Skipton and Settle.

Pro Tip: Check tide schedules and local guidance for river walks; some trails may be slippery after rainfall. Local maps available at stations or visitor centers are essential for safe navigation.

Practical Map for Rail Travelers

- **Step 1:** Train from Leeds → Skipton (1 hour).

- **Step 2:** Walk 5–10 minutes or take a local bus to Skipton town center. Optional exploration: Skipton Castle, canal walks, markets.
- **Step 3:** DalesBus or taxi → Malham, Grassington, Hawes for nature walks, cheese tasting, and village sightseeing.
- **Step 4:** Optional Settle-Carlisle rail journey → view Ribblehead Viaduct and moorlands. Stop at Dent or Appleby for exploration.
- **Step 5:** Return to Skipton by bus/train for onward travel to Leeds, York, or Manchester.

This itinerary allows flexibility, highlights iconic sights, and ensures efficient use of public transport.

The Yorkshire Dales combine breathtaking landscapes with historic villages and a rich food culture, all easily accessible by train. Traveling by rail not only avoids the stress of rural driving but also provides scenic enjoyment en route. Balancing village visits, outdoor walks, and iconic rail journeys ensures a fulfilling experience that captures the essence of this region. Spending at least two days allows immersion in both nature and heritage, making the Dales a truly memorable part of a Britain by Train adventure.

MANCHESTER TO NEWCASTLE: URBAN MEETS COUNTRYSIDE

The journey from Manchester to Newcastle offers one of the most satisfying contrasts in England: bustling industrial cities, historic market towns, and open northern countryside. Traveling by train between these two urban centers allows you to experience dynamic city culture and tranquil rural landscapes without leaving the rail network. This guide details the route, local highlights, cultural experiences, food, seasonal tips, and practical transfers to make the most of a day or overnight rail trip.

PLANNING THE JOURNEY

Train Details

- **Operator:** Avanti West Coast or Northern Rail for direct services between Manchester Piccadilly and Newcastle.
- **Duration:** Direct trains take roughly 2 hours 30 minutes; slower regional services may take 3–3.5 hours but offer more scenic stops.

- **Frequency:** Trains run hourly throughout the day, with additional services at peak times.

Manchester to Newcastle Atlas

Tickets and Classes

- **Advance Tickets:** Book online in advance for lower fares.
- **Off-Peak:** Ideal for mid-morning or early afternoon travel; trains are quieter and more relaxed.
- **First Class:** Offers spacious seating, tables, and complimentary drinks—a great option for enjoying the scenery in comfort.

Travel Tips

- Choose a window seat on the right-hand side for views of the Pennines and rolling countryside leaving Manchester.

- Keep your camera ready: the northern landscapes change quickly, from industrial skylines to wide moorlands.

Manchester: Starting Point

Arrival at Manchester Piccadilly

- Manchester Piccadilly is the main hub for northern and cross-country routes, well-serviced by cafes, newsagents, and luggage facilities.
- If time allows, explore the city before departure. The Northern Quarter offers independent shops, street art, and cafes, while the Science and Industry Museum provide insights into the city's industrial past.

Local Breakfast

- Grab a hearty start at **Evelyn's Café** or **Federal Café & Bar** for locally roasted coffee and breakfast pastries.
- Seasonal tip: In spring, enjoy fresh fruit tarts or local pastries, perfect to take on the train.

MID-MORNING: HEADING INTO COUNTRYSIDE

First Leg: Manchester to Huddersfield

- Departing Manchester, the train heads northeast through Stockport and Stalybridge.
- The route briefly crosses industrial outskirts before opening into rolling green hills as you approach Huddersfield.
- **Huddersfield Station:** A short stop here gives access to the town center, famous for Victorian architecture and the Leeds-Liverpool Canal. Walking through St. George's Square offers views of sandstone buildings and local cafes.

Optional Stop: Holmfirth

- **Access:** Bus from Huddersfield Station (around 30 minutes).
- Holmfirth is known for the filming of *Last of the Summer Wine* and has charming streets, riverside walks, and independent shops.
- Recommended for slow exploration before continuing north.

Late Morning: Through the Pennines

- After Huddersfield, the train climbs into the Pennine hills, often called the "backbone of England."
- Rolling moorlands, stone farmhouses, and small reservoirs dominate the landscape.
- Insight: Take the left-hand side of the train for panoramic views of the moors and distant valleys.

Keighley and Skipton

- **Keighley Station:** A gateway to the Worth Valley, famous for the preserved Keighley & Worth Valley Railway—a heritage steam line through scenic valleys.
- **Skipton Station:** Known as the "Gateway to the Dales," Skipton offers historic market streets, Skipton Castle, and riverside walks. A short 5-minute taxi from the station brings you to the castle and canal.

Lunch: Yorkshire Flavor

- Stop in Skipton for a traditional pub lunch. Options include **The Woolly Sheep** or riverside pubs serving local ales and seasonal dishes.
- Recommended: Roast beef with Yorkshire pudding, locally sourced vegetables, and a pint of Yorkshire ale.
- Seasonal tip: Spring lamb or autumn root vegetable pies showcase the region's fresh produce.

Afternoon: Northumberland and the Approach to Newcastle

Crossing into Northumberland

- Leaving Yorkshire, the train passes through Durham, a city known for its cathedral and riverside views.
- **Durham Station:** A short walk (10–15 minutes) or bus ride to the city center allows exploration of the UNESCO World Heritage Cathedral and Castle.
- Walking along the river provides excellent photo opportunities, particularly in spring when the surrounding greenery is vibrant.

Countryside Views

- After Durham, the landscape becomes more open and gently rolling as you enter Northumberland's fringe. Farm fields, scattered villages, and woodland areas provide a peaceful contrast to the industrial north.
- Seasonal note: Autumn offers golden fields and early sunset lighting, ideal for photography.

ARRIVAL IN NEWCASTLE

Newcastle Central Station

- Located in the city center, the station is a hub for regional and cross-country trains. It is within walking distance of major attractions.
- Upon arrival, explore Grainger Town's neoclassical architecture, the Quayside, and the iconic Tyne Bridge.

Evening Stroll and Dining

- Walk along the Quayside for views of the River Tyne and illuminated bridges.
- Recommended restaurants include **The Broad Chare** for local seafood and **Peace & Loaf** for creative British cuisine.
- Personal Insight: A pint in a traditional pub like **The Bridge Tavern** offers a cozy end to the day, especially in winter months.

Cultural Highlights Along the Route

- **Industrial Heritage:** Manchester, Huddersfield, and Durham all feature museums and architecture reflecting England's industrial past.
- **Heritage Railways:** Keighley & Worth Valley Railway offers steam train excursions through Yorkshire valleys, perfect for photography or family trips.
- **Historic Architecture:** Skipton Castle, Durham Cathedral, and Newcastle's Quayside offer a mix of medieval, Victorian, and neoclassical architecture.

Practical Travel Advice

- **Transfers:** Use local buses or taxis for villages not directly served by rail. Most stations provide clear signage for connections.

- **Walking:** Stations are typically within 10–15 minutes' walk of town centers; cobbled streets and hills may require comfortable shoes.
- **Luggage:** Bring a light daypack with water, snacks, and camera; larger suitcases can be stored in overhead racks on trains.
- **Connectivity:** Wi-Fi is available on most intercity trains; rural sections may have limited signal.

Slow Travel Experience

This route perfectly combines urban energy with peaceful countryside. The contrast between Manchester's vibrant culture and Newcastle's historic charm is framed by scenic hills and valleys, small villages, and heritage towns. Traveling by train allows for observation, photography, and spontaneous exploration—ideal for travelers seeking a blend of city life and northern England's natural beauty.

- Take time to explore each stop rather than rushing; the journey itself is part of the experience.
- Enjoy on-train views as much as the towns: rolling hills, reservoirs, and moorland skies create a dynamic landscape rarely seen from roads.
- Seasonal eating and local pubs enhance the slow travel approach, letting you taste the region as well as see it.

A train journey from Manchester to Newcastle is more than a commute; it's a scenic exploration of northern England. From Manchester's industrial energy through Huddersfield and the Pennines, to the historic streets of Durham and Newcastle, each stop offers cultural, culinary, and natural highlights. By blending direct trains with short local transfers, gentle walks, and seasonal dining, travelers can experience both urban vibrancy and countryside serenity. This route is ideal for those seeking a full northern England experience in a single day or extended rail adventure.

CHAPTER 5
SCOTLAND'S HIGHLANDS & WILDERNESS BY RAIL

Scotland's Highlands are known for their breathtaking landscapes, dramatic mountains, shimmering lochs, and remote villages. These wild and untamed regions are steeped in history, legend, and culture, making them one of the most captivating areas to explore in the UK. Traveling by train offers a unique opportunity to immerse yourself in the rugged beauty of the Scottish Highlands while enjoying the comfort and efficiency of rail travel.

This guide will take you through the best train routes to Scotland's Highlands, offering tips on must-see destinations, local culture, food, and seasonal advice to help you make the most of your journey.

Scotland's most remote railway adventure

GETTING TO SCOTLAND'S HIGHLANDS BY TRAIN

Scotland's rail network offers an excellent way to reach the Highlands, with several iconic routes that provide spectacular views of the countryside. The trains are well-connected, allowing easy access from cities like Edinburgh, Glasgow, and Inverness to the more remote corners of the region.

- **Edinburgh to Inverness**: The journey from Edinburgh to Inverness takes about 3.5 hours, passing through some of Scotland's most stunning landscapes, including the Cairngorms National Park. Trains depart regularly from Edinburgh Waverley Station, offering a comfortable and scenic route into the heart of the Highlands.

- **Glasgow to Mallaig**: One of the most famous train journeys in the world, the West Highland Line from Glasgow to Mallaig offers some of the most dramatic landscapes in Scotland. The journey takes around 5 hours, but the views of lochs, mountains, and the famous Glenfinnan Viaduct (featured in the Harry Potter films) make it well worth the time.

- **Inverness to Kyle of Lochalsh**: The train ride from Inverness to Kyle of Lochalsh is another stunning route, taking about 2.5 hours and passing through the rugged Highlands. Along the way, you'll cross the spectacular Beauly Firth and enjoy views of the Isle of Skye and the surrounding coastline.

- **Fort William to Mallaig**: For those looking to explore the remote beauty of the West Coast, the Jacobite Steam Train operates between Fort William and Mallaig, offering a nostalgic experience on the same route used for the Hogwarts Express in the Harry Potter films.

HIGHLIGHTS OF THE SCOTTISH HIGHLANDS BY RAIL

Inverness: Gateway to the Highlands

Inverness is often referred to as the "Capital of the Highlands." Located at the mouth of the River Ness, this bustling city offers a perfect base from which to explore the surrounding Highlands. From Inverness, you can take a short trip to Loch Ness, one of Scotland's most famous and mysterious lakes.

- **Must-See Attractions**: Visit the Inverness Castle and its beautiful gardens, or explore the Culloden Battlefield, the site of the last major battle fought on British soil. For a taste of local history, check out the Highland Archive Centre or take a walk along the river to the Ness Islands, a peaceful oasis right in the heart of the city.

- **Day Trips from Inverness**: From Inverness, you can easily reach the nearby Cairngorms National Park, known for its dramatic mountain scenery, or venture further north to the remote Isle of Skye.

The West Highland Line: From Glasgow to Mallaig

The West Highland Line is one of the most scenic train routes in the world. This 5-hour journey from Glasgow to Mallaig takes you through the heart of the Scottish Highlands, offering magnificent views of mountains, glens, lochs, and coastal landscapes.8

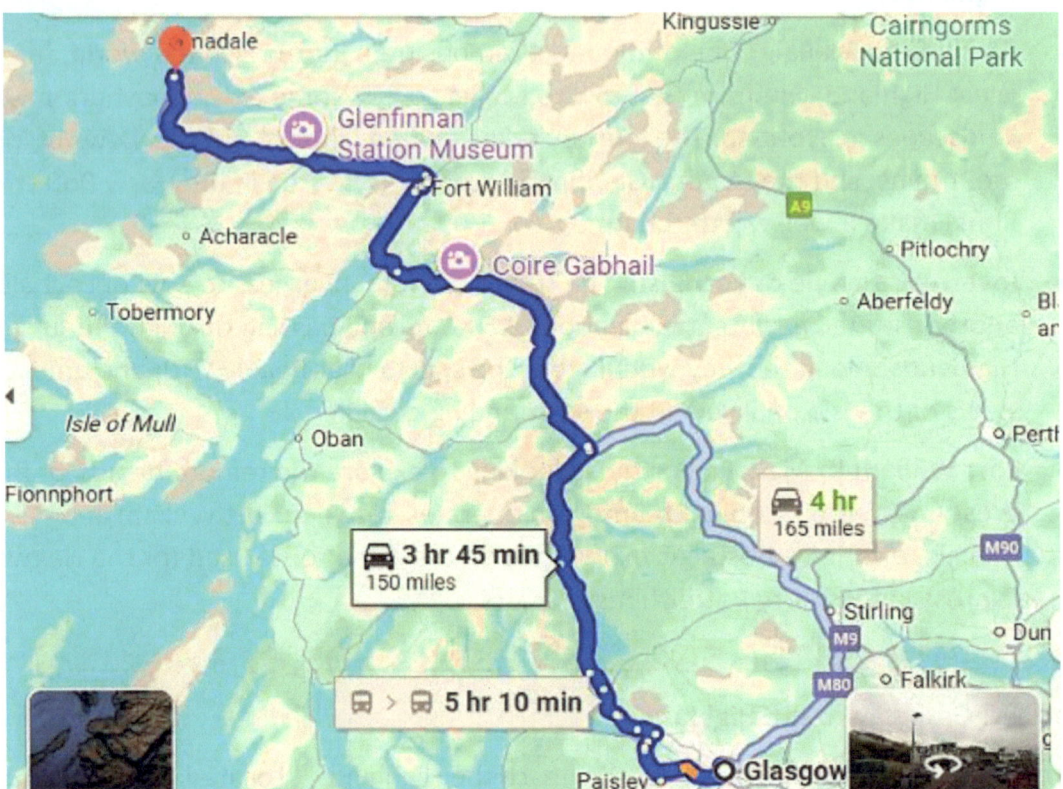

- **Glenfinnan Viaduct**: One of the highlights of this journey is the famous Glenfinnan Viaduct, a 21-arch bridge that crosses the River Finnan. The viaduct was made famous by the Harry Potter films, where it served as the route for the Hogwarts Express. The best views of the viaduct are from the platform at Glenfinnan Station, where you can take a short walk to view the train crossing.

- **Mallaig**: At the end of the journey, Mallaig is a small fishing village on the edge of the Atlantic Ocean. Take a stroll around the harbor, where you can see fishermen at work, or take a boat trip to explore nearby islands such as the Isle of Skye or the Small Isles. Mallaig is also known for its excellent seafood, especially fresh lobster and langoustine.

Loch Ness & Urquhart Castle

A short train ride from Inverness takes you to Loch Ness, one of the most famous and picturesque locations in Scotland. The loch is shrouded in mystery, not only for its size (it is the largest body of freshwater in Scotland by volume) but also for the legendary Loch Ness Monster, Nessie.

- **Urquhart Castle**: On the shores of Loch Ness, Urquhart Castle offers spectacular views of the loch and surrounding hills. The castle itself is a ruin, but it still has a majestic presence, especially when viewed from the water. You can take a boat tour around the loch to learn about the history and mystery of the area.
- **Exploring the Loch**: In addition to visiting the castle, you can also explore the Great Glen Way, a long-distance walking route that runs along the shores of Loch Ness, offering incredible views of the water and its surrounding hills.

THE ISLE OF SKYE: SCOTLAND'S RUGGED BEAUTY

The Isle of Skye is one of Scotland's most popular destinations, known for its rugged landscapes, dramatic cliffs, and picturesque villages. From Kyle of Lochalsh, a small town connected to Skye by the Skye Bridge, you can explore the island's highlights by foot or car.

- **Portree**: The capital of Skye, Portree is a picturesque village with colorful houses lining the harbor. Visit the town's shops and cafes or take a boat trip around the island's coastline to enjoy views of the jagged cliffs and hidden coves.
- **Fairy Pools**: The Fairy Pools, located near Glen Brittle, are a series of crystal-clear pools at the foot of the Black Cuillin mountains. These pools are perfect for a swim or a photography session, especially when the sun sets and the water turns a magical shade of blue.
- **Old Man of Storr**: One of the most iconic landmarks on Skye, the Old Man of Storr is a rock formation that rises dramatically from the surrounding landscape. A challenging but rewarding hike will take you to the top, where you'll be treated to panoramic views of the island.

Local Culture and Food

One of the delights of traveling through the Scottish Highlands by train is the opportunity to enjoy local food and drink. Scotland's Highlands offer a variety of traditional dishes, from hearty stews to freshly caught seafood.

- **Haggis**: Scotland's national dish, haggis, is made from sheep's heart, liver, and lungs, mixed with oats and spices. It's traditionally served with "neeps and tatties" (turnips and potatoes) and is a must-try for adventurous eaters.
- **Seafood**: The Highlands are famous for their seafood, especially shellfish. In places like Mallaig, you can enjoy freshly caught lobster, langoustines, and scallops at local seafood restaurants. Try the *Mallaig Fish and Chip Shop* for some of the best fish and chips in Scotland.
- **Whisky**: No visit to Scotland would be complete without sampling some of its world-renowned whisky. The Highlands is home to many distilleries, and you can find local whiskies at pubs and shops throughout the region. Be sure to stop by a distillery for a guided tour and tasting session.

When to Visit Scotland's Highlands

The best time to visit the Highlands depends on your preferences for weather and activities.

- **Spring and Summer**: These seasons bring mild weather, longer daylight hours, and blooming wildflowers, making them ideal for outdoor activities like hiking, cycling, and sightseeing. The summer months can be busy, so it's best to visit in May or early June if you prefer fewer crowds.
- **Autumn**: Autumn is one of the best times to visit the Highlands, as the foliage turns golden and red, creating stunning landscapes. It's also the time for whisky festivals and harvest celebrations. Temperatures are still mild, but the crowds are fewer than in summer.
- **Winter**: The Highlands in winter are peaceful and serene, with snow-capped mountains and quiet villages. While some roads and paths may be closed due to weather, the winter months offer a unique chance to experience the beauty of Scotland without the usual crowds.

Conclusion: An Unforgettable Journey

Traveling through Scotland's Highlands by rail is an unforgettable experience, offering access to some of the most stunning landscapes in the world. Whether you're enjoying the rugged beauty of the West Highland Line, exploring the mystery of Loch Ness, or soaking in the views from the Isle of Skye, Scotland's rail routes offer a perfect balance of comfort and adventure.

With its rich culture, welcoming communities, and world-class food and drink, the Scottish Highlands are a destination that will leave a lasting impression, whether you're a seasoned traveler or a first-time visitor. So pack your bags, hop on the train, and prepare for an unforgettable journey through one of the most beautiful regions in the UK.

THE WEST HIGHLAND LINE: SCOTLAND'S MOST SCENIC JOURNEY

The **West Highland Line** is widely regarded as one of the most breathtaking rail journeys in Britain. Stretching from **Glasgow Queen Street** through rugged moorlands, lochs, and remote villages to **Mallaig** on Scotland's west coast, this route combines dramatic scenery with accessible Highland culture. Whether you are seeking dramatic mountains, tranquil lochs, historic villages, or fresh seafood, the West Highland Line offers a uniquely immersive experience by train.

The West Highland Line

KEY TRAIN ROUTES AND STATIONS

The main West Highland Line runs from **Glasgow Queen Street** to **Mallaig**, with notable stops including **Garelochhead, Crianlarich, Fort William, Arisaig**, and **Lochailort**. A branch line diverges at Crianlarich, serving **Oban**, a gateway to the Inner Hebrides.

- **Glasgow to Fort William:** About **3 hours 45 minutes**, operated by **ScotRail**, passing through mountains and valleys.
- **Fort William to Mallaig:** Approximately **1 hour 45 minutes**, a highlight for lochside and coastal scenery.
- **Glasgow to Oban:** Around **3 hours**, passing Loch Lomond and the picturesque village of **Tyndrum**.

Tips for Travelers:

- Sit on the right-hand side from Glasgow to Fort William for the best views of **Loch Lomond** and mountains.
- Fort William station is within walking distance of the town center, shops, and visitor services.
- Trains are frequent during the summer, but single-track sections mean careful attention to timetables is essential in winter.

Glasgow: Departure from Scotland's Cultural Hub

Glasgow Queen Street Station is centrally located, near Buchanan Street and George Square. Spend some time exploring the city before departure:

- **Culture & Architecture:** Visit **Glasgow Cathedral**, the **Necropolis**, or the **Kelvingrove Art Gallery and Museum**.
- **Food & Drink:** Glasgow's café scene is vibrant. **Singl-end Coffee** and **The Willow Tea Rooms** offer local flair before you board.
- **Local Insight:** Buying a packed lunch or snacks is advisable; trains to remote areas have limited onboard catering.

Loch Lomond & Trossachs: Rolling Hills and Waterside Villages

After leaving Glasgow, the train passes **Balloch** and enters the **Loch Lomond & The Trossachs National Park**, offering a mix of freshwater lochs, wooded hills, and traditional villages.

- **Dunkeld & Crianlarich:** Small stations provide access to forest walks and historic towns. Crianlarich is a junction for the Oban branch, a good place to stop for supplies or a short hike.

- **Lochside Views:** From **Ardlui to Tyndrum**, the line runs close to lochs and rivers. Keep your camera ready; the views include **Ben More** and surrounding peaks.

On-Foot Options:

- Short walks from station stops provide viewpoints or access to riverside paths.
- In summer, local boat trips on Loch Lomond allow a different perspective.

Rannoch Moor: The Wild Heart of Scotland

Between **Bridge of Orchy** and **Corrour**, the line crosses **Rannoch Moor**, one of Scotland's most dramatic and remote landscapes.

- **Scenery:** Expansive peat bogs, mountains, and occasional wildlife sightings including red deer and golden eagles.
- **Corrour Station:** One of the most remote in the UK, accessible only by train or foot. Ideal for hikers heading to **Loch Ossian** or the surrounding mountains.

Personal Insight: Sitting quietly at a window as the train glides across the moor in early morning light provides one of Scotland's most unforgettable experiences. Winter adds frost and snow, creating a stark but mesmerizing landscape.

Fort William: Outdoor Capital of the Highlands

Fort William is the line's main Highland hub and a gateway to **Ben Nevis**, Britain's tallest mountain.

- **Hiking & Adventure:** Trails range from short riverside walks to full-day ascents of Ben Nevis.
- **Cultural Highlights:** Visit **West Highland Museum** for local history or **Neptune's Staircase** on the Caledonian Canal.
- **Food & Drink:** Try local seafood at **Crannog Seafood Restaurant** or hearty Highland fare at **The Grog & Gruel**.

Transfers:

- Fort William is the starting point for the **Jacobite Steam Train** to Mallaig, made famous as the Hogwarts Express. Reservations are essential.

Mallaig: Coastal Finale

The terminus at Mallaig is a charming fishing village with fresh seafood and ferry connections to the Isles of Skye, Eigg, and Rum.

- **Harbor Walk:** Take a short walk from the station to the harbor for views of fishing boats and the nearby **Arisaig beaches**.
- **Local Cuisine:** Mallaig is famous for fresh shellfish; try the seafood platter at **The West Highland Hotel** or casual fish and chips at harbor-front cafes.
- **Exploration:** Short hikes along coastal paths or a ferry ride to Skye provide memorable outdoor experiences.

Seasonal Tip: Summer offers long daylight hours and boat trips; winter is quieter but atmospheric, with fewer tourists and dramatic skies.

Arisaig & Lochailort: Remote Villages and Coastal Beauty

Between Fort William and Mallaig, small stations serve villages such as **Arisaig** and **Lochailort**.

- **Arisaig:** A short walk to sandy beaches and coastal cliffs. Excellent for birdwatching and photography.
- **Lochailort:** Gateway to the West Highland Way and remote walking trails. Cafes and inns are limited, so bring supplies if hiking.

On-Foot Tips: Most stations are less than 10 minutes' walk from village centers. Some paths may be muddy; waterproof boots are recommended.

Seasonal & Practical Considerations

- **Summer (June–August):** Long days, boat trips, and easier access to remote hikes. Popular with tourists; book tickets in advance.
- **Autumn (September–November):** Fewer crowds, colorful foliage, dramatic skies. Be prepared for rain.
- **Winter (December–February):** Snow-dusted mountains and quiet moors; check timetables for reduced service.
- **Spring (March–May):** Early wildflowers, lambs on the hills, and fewer tourists.

Travel Tips:

- Off-peak tickets are cheaper, especially for the Fort William–Mallaig section.
- Bring layers and waterproof clothing; the Highlands are unpredictable.
- Cameras or smartphones are essential; the scenery changes constantly, and many highlights are visible from the train.

Personal Insight

Traveling the West Highland Line feels like entering another world. The contrast between the urban departure in Glasgow and the remote villages and lochs at the route's end is striking. Sitting in a comfortable train carriage while watching the mountains rise, rivers shimmer, and villages appear only briefly creates a meditative, scenic experience. Early morning departures offer mist over lochs and fewer crowds, while evening trains highlight sunsets behind fells.

Insider Tip: Book a window seat early and keep a small backpack with water, snacks, and a camera. Short walks at stops like Corrour or Arisaig provide a break and extra perspective on this stunning region.

The **West Highland Line** combines accessibility, comfort, and unparalleled scenery. From Glasgow's city center to the remote west coast, the journey offers mountains, moors, lochs, historic villages, and cultural insights. Key highlights include **Loch Lomond, Rannoch Moor, Fort William**, and **Mallaig**, with opportunities for hiking, boating, and tasting local cuisine. Seasonal variations enhance the experience, from summer's long daylight to winter's stark landscapes.

This route exemplifies why rail travel in Britain is not just a way to get from A to B, but a **memorable scenic adventure**, blending natural beauty, village life, and Highland culture in a way that is only possible from the train.

EDINBURGH TO INVERNESS: A RIDE THROUGH HISTORY AND NATURE

Traveling from Edinburgh to Inverness by train is one of Britain's most scenic journeys, offering a blend of historic landmarks, Highland landscapes, and cultural experiences. This route takes you through the heart of Scotland, past castles, lochs, and rolling hills, making it ideal for travelers seeking both natural beauty and a taste of Scottish heritage.

Edinburgh to Inverness by train route

By train, you can enjoy the journey without the stress of driving, while stopping at key towns and attractions along the way.

GETTING STARTED: EDINBURGH WAVERLEY STATION

Edinburgh Waverley is Scotland's principal station, centrally located at the east end of Princes Street and adjacent to the historic Old Town.

- **Facilities:** Modern waiting areas, cafés, luggage storage, and ticket offices.

- **Train Services:** ScotRail and LNER operate direct services to Inverness, typically taking 3 hours 20 minutes to 3 hours 40 minutes. Trains offer first-class and standard seating, free Wi-Fi, and panoramic windows for scenic views.

- **Tips for Travel:** Choose a morning train for daylight viewing of the Highlands, particularly through Fife and Perthshire. Booking tickets in advance guarantees window seats, especially in summer.

Personal Insight: Arriving early at Waverley allows a quick stroll along Princes Street Gardens, providing a calm start before boarding and an excellent view of Edinburgh Castle.

The Route and Scenic Highlights

The Edinburgh to Inverness line is as much about the journey as the destination. Key segments include:

- **Edinburgh to Perth:** Rolling farmland, Fife villages, and glimpses of the River Tay. Pass through towns like Kirkcaldy and Dundee, with the Tay Bridge offering dramatic river views.

- **Perth to Aviemore:** The route enters Highland terrain, passing lochs, forests, and mountains. The train follows the River Spey in parts, offering spectacular reflections and wildlife sightings.

- **Aviemore to Inverness:** The final stretch traverses the Cairngorms National Park, with moorlands, pine forests, and occasional glimpses of ancient castles before descending to Inverness and the Moray Firth.

Travel Insight: The left side of the train northbound provides the best views of the Cairngorms and River Spey, while the right side offers open moorlands and Highland villages.

KEY STOPS AND EXPERIENCES ALONG THE WAY

Several towns along the route are worth exploring if you wish to break up the journey:

- **Perth:** Historic city on the banks of the River Tay. Visit Scone Palace, the crowning place of Scottish kings, or stroll along the riverside. A short walk from the station takes you to cafés serving local fare.

- **Pitlochry:** A small Highland town accessible from certain ScotRail services. Ideal for a short stop to explore Victorian streets, the Edradour Distillery (Scotland's smallest traditional distillery), and nearby walks.

- **Aviemore:** A hub for outdoor activities in the Cairngorms. Hiking, mountain biking, or simply enjoying Loch Morlich are highlights. The town also has a range of pubs and cafés serving hearty Highland fare.

Pro Tip: Even if staying on the train, these stops offer great photo opportunities as the train passes. For longer exploration, schedule a few hours or an overnight stay to fully enjoy the area.

Cultural and Historic Highlights

Scotland's history is ever-present along the Edinburgh–Inverness line:

- **Castles and Estates:** Look for Blair Castle, Drum Castle, and Ruthven Barracks along the route. Many are visible from the train or a short walk/taxi ride from nearby stations.
- **Local Culture:** The Highland towns retain traditional Scottish charm with craft shops, woolen goods, and local cafés. Sampling a shortbread or local oatcake in Pitlochry or Aviemore is highly recommended.
- **Festivals:** Summer and autumn feature Highland Games, music festivals, and food events in Pitlochry and Aviemore, providing authentic cultural immersion.

Personal Insight: Passing through the Highlands by train allows a connection with Scotland's history in a way that driving often misses—scenery unfolds gradually, revealing castles, glens, and rivers in natural context.

Food and Dining Options

Onboard dining and local stops provide a range of culinary experiences:

- **Onboard:** Many trains have a buffet car with hot drinks, sandwiches, and snacks. First-class often includes complimentary light meals.
- **Perth:** Riverbank cafés and bakeries offer locally sourced products, including Scottish salmon and oatcakes.
- **Pitlochry and Aviemore:** Distillery tours often include tastings. Local pubs serve traditional dishes such as Cullen skink, venison stew, or haggis with neeps and tatties.
- **Picnic Option:** Pick up cheese, smoked salmon, or pastries at station shops for a scenic picnic while on a longer train segment or at a stopover in the Cairngorms.

Travel Tip: During summer, outdoor dining is pleasant in towns like Pitlochry, where riverside seating enhances the experience.

Seasonal Tips for the Journey

The journey varies dramatically with the seasons, affecting scenery, wildlife, and activity options:

- **Spring (March–May):** Snow melts reveal waterfalls and rivers. Wildflowers bloom along the Cairngorms, making walks ideal.

- **Summer (June–August):** Long days and sunny skies provide optimal views. Outdoor activities and festivals are in full swing. Trains may be busy—advance bookings are essential.

- **Autumn (September–November):** Golden foliage and moorland heather create stunning photography opportunities. Crisp air is perfect for short hikes along the route.

- **Winter (December–February):** Snow-capped peaks and low-light conditions create dramatic vistas. Some train services may have reduced frequency, so plan ahead.

Personal Insight: Autumn and spring are my favorite times for this route—the soft lighting enhances the scenery without the summer crowds.

Walking and Exploration Options Near Stations

Even if your journey is primarily by train, short walks add depth to the experience:

- **Perth Riverside Walks:** 10–20-minute riverside trails offer peaceful scenery with historic bridges and swans on the River Tay.

- **Pitlochry Walks:** Explore the town center and nearby woodland trails in 30–60 minutes. Don't miss the scenic viewpoint near the dam at Pitlochry Hydro-Electric Station.

- **Aviemore Trails:** Short walks along Loch Morlich or the Speyside Way provide accessible routes for casual exploration, with the option for longer hikes in the Cairngorms National Park.

Travel Tip: Wear waterproof footwear in spring or autumn; Highland paths can be muddy after rain.

Arriving in Inverness

Inverness, the capital of the Highlands, marks the end of the journey:

- **Station to City Center:** A 10-minute walk takes you to the riverfront, shops, and Inverness Castle viewpoint. Taxis and buses are also available.
- **Local Highlights:** Explore the Victorian Market, Inverness Cathedral, and riverside walks along the Ness. The city provides excellent access to Loch Ness and surrounding Highland scenery.
- **Dining:** Local pubs and restaurants offer fresh seafood, Highland venison, and modern Scottish cuisine. Inverness is a good base for a multi-day exploration of northern Scotland.

Personal Insight: Arriving in Inverness by train gives a sense of progression through Scotland's landscapes—the city feels like a natural extension of the Highland journey.

Practical Map for Rail Travelers

- **Step 1:** Edinburgh Waverley → Inverness by ScotRail or LNER (3h20–3h40).
- **Step 2:** Optional stop at Perth for Scone Palace and riverside walks (short walk from station).
- **Step 3:** Optional stop at Pitlochry for distillery tours, Victorian streets, and woodland walks.
- **Step 4:** Optional stop at Aviemore for hiking, cycling, or Loch Morlich.
- **Step 5:** Continue to Inverness. Walk 10 minutes or take local transport to city highlights, hotels, or riverside restaurants.

This itinerary balances a scenic train journey with optional exploration stops, making the most of Scotland's natural beauty and heritage.

Traveling by rail from Edinburgh to Inverness is both practical and immersive, combining Scotland's history, culture, and natural splendor. The route offers iconic landscapes, charming towns, and access to the Highlands without the stress of driving. Planning for daylight travel, seasonal conditions, and key stopovers enhances the experience, allowing a full appreciation of castles, rivers, mountains, and traditional Scottish life. Whether for a one-day scenic ride or an extended Highland adventure, this journey offers some of the most memorable rail travel in Britain.

SKYE & LOCH NESS: MAJESTIC LANDSCAPES AND LEGENDS

The Scottish Highlands offer some of Britain's most dramatic scenery, combining rugged mountains, deep lochs, and misty moors. A journey to Skye and Loch Ness by train blends scenic rail travel with small-town exploration, local culture, and legendary landscapes. This guide provides practical advice on train routes, local transfers, walking options, food, seasonal tips, and insider experiences to make the most of your Highland adventure.

Skye, Loch Ness and Inverness Winter Tour

PLANNING YOUR HIGHLAND JOURNEY

Train Routes

- **To Inverness:** Trains from Edinburgh Waverley or Glasgow Queen Street to Inverness take 3.5–4.5 hours. Operated by ScotRail, these routes cross the Cairngorms and Moray Firth, offering scenic views along the way.

- **To Kyle of Lochalsh (Gateway to Skye):** From Inverness, ScotRail runs the Kyle Line through Dingwall, Garve, and Achnasheen to Kyle of Lochalsh. The journey takes about 5 hours and is widely regarded as one of Scotland's most scenic rail routes.

- **Connecting to Skye:** From Kyle of Lochalsh, buses or taxis cross the Skye Bridge to Portree and other villages on the island. Some tours combine rail and local minibuses for easier access to remote spots.

Tickets and Classes

- **Advance Booking:** Essential in summer for Kyle Line trains; seats can sell out quickly.
- **ScotRail Mobile App:** Useful for real-time updates, tickets, and platform information.
- **First Class:** Offers wider seats, tables, and views of the passing Highlands—ideal for photography and comfort on long routes.

Morning: Inverness Arrival and Loch Ness Exploration

Inverness Station

- Inverness is compact and walkable. From the station, taxis or buses can take you to the city center in 5 minutes.
- If time allows, explore the Victorian Market and riverside streets. Breakfast at **Velocity Café & Bicycle Workshop** or **The Castle Café** offers hearty Scottish fare and strong coffee.

Loch Ness by Train and Bus

- From Inverness, take a ScotRail train to **Achnagarry or Fort Augustus via local bus connections**—note that direct train service to Fort Augustus is limited, so a combination of rail to Inverness outskirts and bus is often needed.
- Loch Ness is most famous for its legendary monster, but the area also offers forests, waterfalls, and gentle hiking trails.
- **Walking Insight:** Fort Augustus pier is ideal for a short riverside walk, and the Caledonian Canal provides flat trails with scenic loch views.

Jacobite Steam Train Tour from Inverness

Lunch

- Pubs and cafes along the loch serve fresh trout or salmon, often accompanied by roasted root vegetables.
- Seasonal tip: In autumn, local venison dishes are common. For a lighter option, packed sandwiches or locally made pies are ideal for loch-side picnics.

Afternoon: Journey to Skye

Kyle of Lochalsh Scenic Rail

- Board the Kyle Line at Inverness for a journey through the Highlands to Kyle of Lochalsh.
- **Highlights:**
    - The Cromarty Firth near Dingwall offers wide views of water and distant hills.
    - Past Garve, the line enters remote wilderness with rivers, lochs, and heather moors.

- Eilean Donan Castle, visible from the train near Kyle of Lochalsh, is one of Scotland's most photographed castles.
- Personal Insight: Sitting on the left-hand side provides unobstructed views of the Highlands. Keep your camera ready; the scenery shifts rapidly from farmland to mountains.

Kyle of Lochalsh to Portree

- From Kyle, buses cross the Skye Bridge to Portree, the island's capital. The bus takes 45 minutes along dramatic coastal roads with frequent stops for viewpoints.
- Optional taxi transfers are faster and allow flexible stops at scenic points like Broadford or Sligachan.

Evening: Skye Exploration

Portree

- Portree is a compact town with a picturesque harbor, colorful houses, and walking paths along the cliffs.
- Walk along the harbor to enjoy local art galleries and craft shops. Stop at **The Granary** or **Café Arriba** for coffee or early dinner.
- Seasonal Insight: Summer evenings are long and ideal for cliff walks; in winter, sunset occurs as early as 3:30 pm, so plan late-afternoon hikes carefully.

Dinner

- Seafood dominates Skye's cuisine. Try langoustines, fresh scallops, or locally caught cod at **Scorrybreac** or **Sea Breezes**.
- Pair with a Scottish ale or a dram of local whisky for a Highland experience.

Cultural and Natural Highlights

Eilean Donan Castle

- Visible from the train near Kyle of Lochalsh, this restored 13th-century castle sits at the junction of three lochs.
- A short walk around the grounds provides photographic opportunities and insight into Highland history.

The Cuillin Mountains

- Accessible by bus or taxi from Portree, the Cuillins offer hiking for all levels, from gentle glen walks to steep mountain paths.
- Personal Insight: Early morning or late afternoon light highlights the mountains' dramatic ridges; even short walks reveal waterfalls and loch-side reflections.

Loch Ness Legend

- Local tours often combine historical storytelling with scenic walks. Even without spotting Nessie, the loch's mirrored waters and surrounding hills create a magical atmosphere.
- Small villages along the loch, like Invermoriston or Drumnadrochit, feature craft shops and museums detailing folklore and geology.

Seasonal Tips

- **Spring:** Wildflowers bloom in Glen Shiel and along the Skye coastal paths; loch waters are clear and reflective.
- **Summer:** Long daylight hours allow extended walks and evening photography. Book accommodations and trains in advance.
- **Autumn:** Golden moorland and fewer tourists make this ideal for a quieter visit. Watch for early sunset and pack layers.
- **Winter:** Snow-dusted peaks and mist over the lochs create atmospheric photography opportunities, but some bus routes may be reduced. Dress warmly and plan daylight excursions carefully.

Practical Travel Advice

- **Transfers:** Bus connections and taxis are essential for reaching remote villages or hikes on Skye. Timetables can be sparse outside peak season, so check in advance.
- **Walking:** Wear sturdy boots; many paths near lochs and mountains can be boggy or uneven.
- **Packing:** Daypacks should include water, snacks, waterproof layers, and a camera. Even summer weather can be unpredictable.

- **Connectivity:** Mobile signal is intermittent in remote Highlands, so download maps and train/bus schedules beforehand.

Slow Travel Experience

Traveling to Skye and Loch Ness by train and bus allows a pace that encourages observation and reflection. Rolling countryside, sparkling lochs, and coastal cliffs unfold gradually, giving travelers time to immerse themselves in Highland culture and natural beauty. Walking along quiet paths, stopping at small cafes, or photographing reflections on a loch enhances the sense of connection with the landscape.

- Embrace local hospitality in pubs and tearooms. Sampling seafood, game, and locally brewed ale enriches the travel experience.
- Combine rail and bus strategically to access hidden gems like Sligachan, Elgol, or small villages along the loch shores.
- Even brief hikes along loch shores or mountain glens reward travelers with panoramic views that linger long after the journey.

A train-and-bus journey through the Scottish Highlands to Skye and Loch Ness combines dramatic scenery, local culture, and legendary landscapes. Start with Inverness and Loch Ness, exploring castles, riverside paths, and folklore. Continue along the Kyle Line to Kyle of Lochalsh, absorbing mountain views, rivers, and historic villages. Finally, cross to Skye to enjoy Portree, coastal walks, and the Cuillin Mountains. Seasonal planning, practical transfers, and an emphasis on slow travel allow visitors to experience the Highlands fully, combining comfort, adventure, and the sense of timelessness that defines northern Scotland.

CHAPTER 6
WALES: MOUNTAINS, COASTLINES & CASTLES BY TRAIN

Wales is a land of extraordinary contrasts, where towering mountains meet rugged coastlines, and ancient castles dot the landscape. From the sweeping vistas of Snowdonia National Park to the pristine beaches of Pembrokeshire, this small but stunning country offers a wealth of natural beauty and historical charm, all accessible by rail. Whether you're an outdoor enthusiast, a history buff, or someone looking for a peaceful getaway, Wales provides a memorable and easily navigable rail experience.

In this section, we'll guide you through some of the best train routes in Wales, showcasing its most iconic destinations, hidden gems, cultural highlights, and the best times to visit.

One-week Borders and Wales by train itinerary

Getting to Wales by Train

Wales is well-connected to the rest of the UK, with direct train routes from major cities like London, Manchester, and Birmingham. The country's rail network is efficient, offering regular services to the cities, towns, and natural wonders that make Wales a must-visit destination.

- **London to Cardiff**: Trains from London Paddington to Cardiff take around 2 hours, making it a perfect base for exploring southern Wales. From Cardiff, you can take trains to other key locations, such as Swansea or the Pembrokeshire coast.

- **London to Snowdonia**: Reaching Snowdonia National Park by train takes a bit longer, but the journey is well worth it. The train from London Euston to Bangor takes about 3.5 hours, and from Bangor, you can catch a local train to scenic locations like Betws-y-Coed or Caernarfon.

- **Manchester to Aberystwyth**: From Manchester Piccadilly, a 3-hour train ride takes you to Aberystwyth, a charming seaside town on the west coast, serving as a great base for exploring the mountains and coastline of mid-Wales.

HIGHLIGHTS OF WALES BY RAIL

Cardiff: Capital of Culture and History

Cardiff, the capital of Wales, is a vibrant and modern city that is also rich in history and culture. A train journey from London takes you into the heart of this dynamic city, where you can explore everything from ancient castles to modern art galleries.

stunning sights from one of Wales

- **Cardiff Castle**: Situated in the city center, Cardiff Castle is one of Wales' most iconic landmarks. Dating back to Roman times, the castle offers a fascinating glimpse into the country's history. Explore the medieval fortifications, lavish Victorian interiors, and the beautiful grounds.
- **Bute Park**: For a dose of nature in the city, visit Bute Park, a large parkland located right next to Cardiff Castle. This green space is ideal for a relaxing walk, and it features the beautiful Sophia Gardens and the River Taff running through it.
- **Cardiff Bay**: Cardiff Bay is home to the Wales Millennium Centre, an architectural marvel that hosts world-class performances. The area also offers an array of waterfront restaurants, bars, and cafes. A boat trip around the bay provides a different perspective of this lively area.
- **Cultural Scene**: Cardiff is also known for its cultural attractions. The National Museum Cardiff showcases Welsh art, geology, and natural history, while the St. David's Hall hosts performances ranging from classical music to contemporary shows.

Snowdonia National Park: A Hiker's Paradise

Snowdonia, located in the heart of North Wales, is a paradise for outdoor enthusiasts. The park is home to some of the UK's highest peaks, including Mount Snowdon, and offers countless trails, lakes, and valleys to explore. Trains from London and Manchester provide easy access to this rugged wilderness, where you can enjoy everything from challenging hikes to serene lakeside strolls.

- **Snowdon Mountain Railway**: If hiking to the summit of Snowdon (Wales' highest peak) isn't your thing, the Snowdon Mountain Railway offers a scenic train ride up the mountain. The 4.5-mile journey takes you through spectacular views of the surrounding valleys, and on a clear day, you can see all the way to Ireland.
- **Betws-y-Coed**: This charming village is the gateway to Snowdonia National Park. Surrounded by dense forests and tranquil rivers, it's a popular spot for hiking, climbing, and photography. From here, you can easily access several trails that lead into the mountains or visit nearby attractions like Swallow Falls, a dramatic cascade of water.

- **Caernarfon Castle**: A short train ride from Snowdonia, Caernarfon Castle is one of Wales' most impressive medieval structures. This UNESCO World Heritage site was the birthplace of Prince Charles and is known for its massive walls and polygonal towers. The castle is a must-see for history lovers and those interested in Welsh heritage.

THE PEMBROKESHIRE COAST: WILD BEACHES AND SCENIC VILLAGES

Wales' southwest coast is home to some of the most beautiful and unspoiled beaches in the UK, along with charming villages and rugged cliffs. Traveling by train from Cardiff or Swansea to the Pembrokeshire coast allows you to explore the area's natural beauty and rich maritime history.

Pembrokeshire coast trail

- **St. Davids**: As the smallest city in the UK, St. Davids offers a peaceful escape from the hustle and bustle of everyday life. Visit St. Davids Cathedral, an architectural masterpiece set against a dramatic landscape, and explore the surrounding coastal paths that lead to stunning views of the Atlantic Ocean.

- **Pembroke Castle**: Located in the town of Pembroke, this massive Norman castle is a fantastic example of medieval military architecture. Visitors can explore the castle's dungeons, towers, and ramparts while learning about its pivotal role in Welsh history.

- **Barafundle Bay**: Known for its golden sand and crystal-clear waters, Barafundle Bay is one of Pembrokeshire's most beautiful beaches. It's accessible via a half-mile walk from the nearest car park, making it a serene and secluded spot for a day out.
- **Tenby**: The seaside town of Tenby is one of the most picturesque in Wales, with its colorful buildings, sandy beaches, and cobbled streets. The town is perfect for a relaxing day spent exploring or enjoying the local seafood, especially freshly caught crab and lobster.

Local Culture and Food

Wales is a land with a rich cultural heritage, and this is reflected in the country's food, music, and festivals. Traveling by train provides an opportunity to sample some of the best local dishes, whether you're stopping for a meal in a quaint village café or enjoying a pint in a traditional Welsh pub.

- **Welsh Cawl**: A traditional Welsh dish, cawl is a hearty lamb stew made with vegetables like leeks, potatoes, and carrots. It's the perfect meal after a long day of hiking in the mountains or exploring the countryside.
- **Welsh Rarebit**: This beloved Welsh comfort food consists of a rich, cheesy sauce served over toasted bread. It's often served as a snack or light meal and is a must-try for visitors looking for authentic Welsh cuisine.
- **Ffresh Food and Drink**: Many of Wales' best restaurants focus on using local, seasonal ingredients. In Cardiff, try *The Potted Pig* for a modern take on Welsh food, or head to *The Shed* in Aberystwyth for fresh seafood caught straight from the coast.
- **Welsh Music and Festivals**: Wales has a strong musical tradition, from its famous male choirs to its folk music. Be sure to check out a local performance, and if you're in the country during the summer, look for festivals like the *National Eisteddfod*, which celebrates Welsh culture through music, poetry, and dance.

When to Visit Wales

Wales is a year-round destination, with each season offering something different.

- **Spring and Summer**: These seasons bring warmer weather and longer days, ideal for hiking, cycling, and exploring Wales' national parks and coastline. However, popular tourist spots can get busy, so consider traveling early in the season or during the weekdays for a quieter experience.

- **Autumn**: Autumn is a wonderful time to visit Wales, as the landscapes turn golden and the weather remains mild. The National Eisteddfod is held in August, and the autumn harvest offers opportunities to enjoy seasonal Welsh dishes and local festivals.

- **Winter**: If you're after a quieter, more peaceful visit, winter is a great time to explore Wales. The cities and coastal villages are far less crowded, and the rugged landscapes of the mountains and beaches look even more dramatic when dusted with snow.

Wales offers an incredible variety of landscapes, experiences, and cultural riches, all accessible by rail. From the majestic peaks of Snowdonia to the sandy shores of Pembrokeshire and the vibrant streets of Cardiff, the country's scenic train routes provide a relaxed and convenient way to explore its treasures. Whether you're seeking adventure, history, or just a peaceful escape, Wales is a destination that promises to leave a lasting impression. So, hop on the train, sit back, and let the beauty of Wales unfold before you.

CONWY TO SNOWDONIA: A JOURNEY THROUGH WELSH HISTORY

Traveling by train from **Conwy** into the heart of **Snowdonia** offers a blend of medieval history, rugged mountains, and picturesque villages. North Wales is rich in heritage, and the railways provide a relaxing, scenic way to access castles, hiking trails, and lakes without the stress of driving winding mountain roads. This route is ideal for history enthusiasts, hikers, and anyone seeking a true Welsh cultural experience.

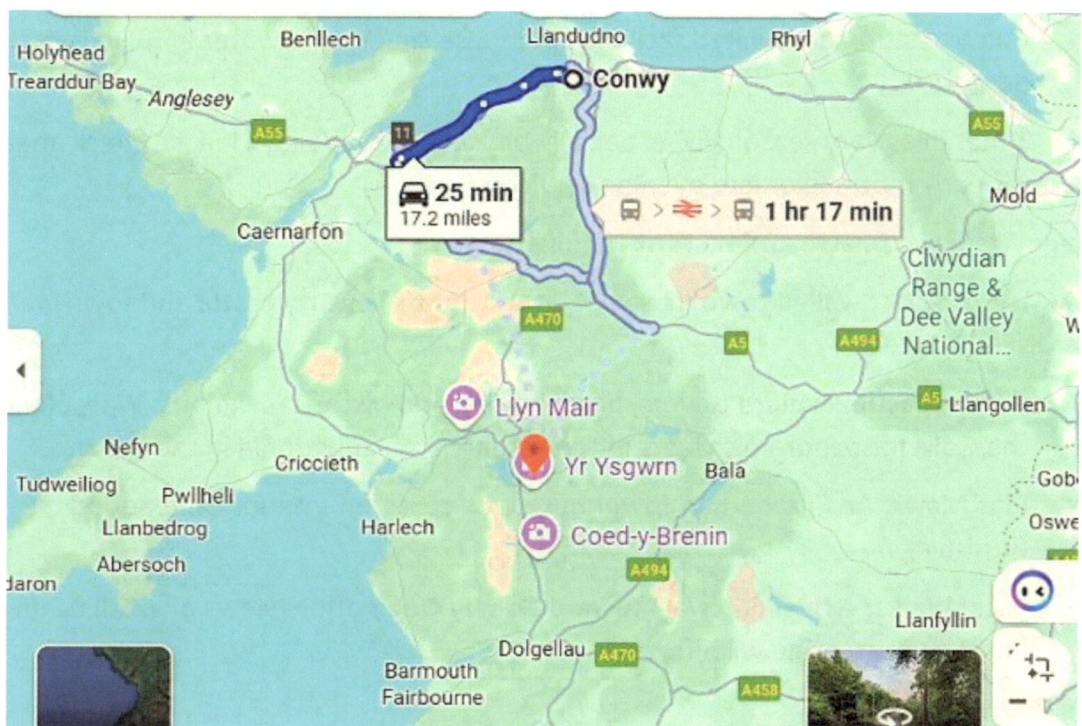

Conwy to Snowdonia train route

KEY TRAIN ROUTES AND CONNECTIONS

The journey begins at **Conwy Station**, a short walk from the town center and Conwy Castle. The main rail connections for Snowdonia include:

- **Conwy to Bangor:** Operated by **Transport for Wales**, this scenic section hugs the **Conwy estuary** with views of mountains across the water. Travel time is around **30 minutes**, with multiple daily services.

- **Bangor to Llandudno Junction:** The line continues along the coast, providing access to **Llandudno** for seaside charm before connecting to the **Conwy Valley Line** toward Snowdonia.

- **Llandudno Junction to Blaenau Ffestiniog:** The **Conwy Valley Line** runs through dramatic landscapes, including river valleys, small villages, and the outskirts of **Snowdonia National Park**, in approximately **1 hour 15 minutes**.

Practical Tips:

- Seat on the right-hand side when traveling north for the best estuary and mountain views.

- Conwy Station has limited facilities; purchase snacks and water in town before departure.
- Timetables vary seasonally, especially on the Conwy Valley Line, so check ahead for early morning or late evening services.

Conwy: Medieval Charm and Historic Highlights

Conwy is a compact walled town, renowned for its **13th-century castle** and town walls, both UNESCO-listed.

- **Conwy Castle:** Explore towers, battlements, and historical exhibits. Walk along the walls for panoramic views of the estuary and Snowdonia in the distance.
- **Plas Mawr:** An Elizabethan townhouse with restored interiors and period furnishings.
- **Local Walks:** A riverside walk toward **Conwy Quay** offers views of small fishing boats and estuarine wildlife.

Food & Drink:

- **The Erskine Arms:** Classic Welsh pub fare, including lamb and seafood.
- **Caffi Conwy:** Serves light lunches, tea, and local pastries—perfect for a pre-train snack.

Seasonal Tip: Spring and summer are ideal for outdoor exploration of walls and quay; autumn offers crisp air and fewer crowds.

LLANDUDNO JUNCTION AND COASTAL CHARM

A short train ride or local bus takes you to **Llandudno Junction**, a practical interchange to the **Conwy Valley Line**. Nearby **Llandudno**, the Victorian seaside town, is a worthwhile detour:

- **Promenade & Pier:** Stroll along a classic Victorian promenade with cafes, ice cream stalls, and pier arcades.
- **Great Orme Tramway:** Offers views over the Irish Sea and the town, easily accessible from the center.

Llandudno Junction coastal charm

Food & Drink:

- **The Cottage Loaf:** Casual café with locally sourced sandwiches and cakes.
- **Mostyn Brewery:** Small craft brewery offering tasting sessions of local ales.

The Conwy Valley Line: Scenic Rail into Snowdonia

The **Conwy Valley Line** winds from Llandudno Junction to **Blaenau Ffestiniog**, crossing rivers, wooded valleys, and the edges of Snowdonia.

- **Key Villages:**
    - **Betws-y-Coed:** Station located within walking distance of the village, gateway to forests and waterfalls. Visit **Swallow Falls** and **Conwy Valley trails**.
    - **Capel Curig:** Surrounded by mountains and fells, offering short hikes and lakeside walks.
    - **Dolwyddelan:** Medieval castle nearby, accessible on foot from the station via a short uphill walk.

On-Foot Tips:

- Many stations are within 10–15 minutes' walk of village centers and trailheads.
- Trails vary from gentle riverside walks to more challenging climbs; sturdy boots are essential.

Scenic Insight:

- The view of **Snowdon Massif** approaching Blaenau Ffestiniog is spectacular, particularly in the early morning light. Winter may feature snow-capped peaks, enhancing photography.

BLAENAU FFESTINIOG: SLATE HISTORY AND MOUNTAIN ACCESS

Blaenau Ffestiniog, at the end of the Conwy Valley Line, is a historic slate-mining town surrounded by dramatic mountains.

- **Ffestiniog Railway:** Connects to Porthmadog and offers a narrow-gauge heritage rail experience through forests and tunnels.
- **Outdoor Activities:** Hiking trails start from the station, including routes to **Moelwyn Mawr** and **Cwmorthin quarry paths**.
- **Local Cuisine:** Small cafes such as **Caffi Gwynant** provide light meals and Welsh cakes.

Personal Insight: Hiking from Blaenau Ffestiniog into Snowdonia offers a quieter experience than the busier Snowdon paths from Llanberis. Early morning departures allow you to enjoy the mountains before crowds arrive.

Cultural and Seasonal Highlights

- **Heritage:** North Wales' castles, slate towns, and medieval villages provide a deep sense of history along this route.
- **Festivals:** Look for local events, such as Betws-y-Coed's summer craft fairs or Blaenau Ffestiniog's slate mining heritage celebrations.
- **Cuisine:** Sample lamb, locally caught fish, and traditional Welsh cakes. Pubs in smaller villages often offer locally brewed ales.
- **Photography & Wildlife:** The route passes rivers, forests, and mountain valleys. Wild red kites, deer, and otters are occasionally spotted along the Conwy River.

Seasonal Notes:

- **Spring:** Wildflowers and newborn lambs enhance village walks.
- **Summer:** Longer daylight for exploring castles, villages, and walking trails.
- **Autumn:** Vibrant foliage in forests and river valleys.
- **Winter:** Snow-dusted peaks and fewer tourists, but check train times carefully.

Practical Travel Tips

- **Tickets:** Book in advance via National Rail or Transport for Wales for discounted fares.
- **Connections:** Check local bus and taxi services in villages for onward access to castles, lakes, and trailheads.
- **Walking Gear:** Waterproof boots, layers, and a small backpack with water and snacks are recommended.
- **Photography:** Window seats on the right-hand side provide the best views of the estuary, rivers, and mountains heading north.

Local Insight: Trains run at a leisurely pace, allowing travelers to enjoy the scenery. For those seeking more adventure, alighting at Betws-y-Coed or Capel Curig and walking through forest trails provides a memorable Highland experience without the crowds.

Personal Insight

Traveling from **Conwy to Blaenau Ffestiniog** by train feels like moving through centuries of Welsh history. Medieval castles, slate villages, and riverside towns pass in sequence, framed by the dramatic backdrop of Snowdonia. Stopping at small stations to explore forests, waterfalls, and mountain trails creates a sense of immersion. I recommend an early departure from Conwy to maximize daylight in the valleys and reach Blaenau Ffestiniog in time for a scenic hike.

The combination of medieval architecture, local culture, and accessible hiking makes this journey ideal for travelers who want both history and natural beauty in one trip.

The **Conwy to Snowdonia journey** combines rail convenience, rich heritage, and breathtaking scenery. From Conwy's medieval walls to the remote villages and rugged peaks of Snowdonia, the route provides access to castles, rivers, lakes, and hiking trails—all within reach of small stations. Seasonal awareness enhances every stop:

spring wildflowers, summer long days, autumnal color, and snow-dusted peaks in winter.

This rail journey exemplifies why North Wales is best explored by train: stress-free travel, direct access to historic sites, immersive scenery, and opportunities for walking and cultural experiences that reveal the heart of Welsh history and natural beauty.

THE BRECON BEACONS: EXPLORE BY TRAIN AND FOOT

The Brecon Beacons National Park, located in South Wales, is a landscape of rolling hills, rugged mountains, cascading waterfalls, and historic market towns. Traveling by train to the Brecon Beacons allows visitors to enjoy scenic Welsh countryside while minimizing the stress of rural driving. From historic rail lines to walking trails, local pubs, and cultural highlights, this guide provides everything a traveler needs to explore the Brecon Beacons efficiently and memorably.

Exploring the Brecon Beacons

GETTING TO THE BRECON BEACONS BY TRAIN

The Brecon Beacons are accessible from major Welsh and English cities, though some connections require short bus or taxi transfers:

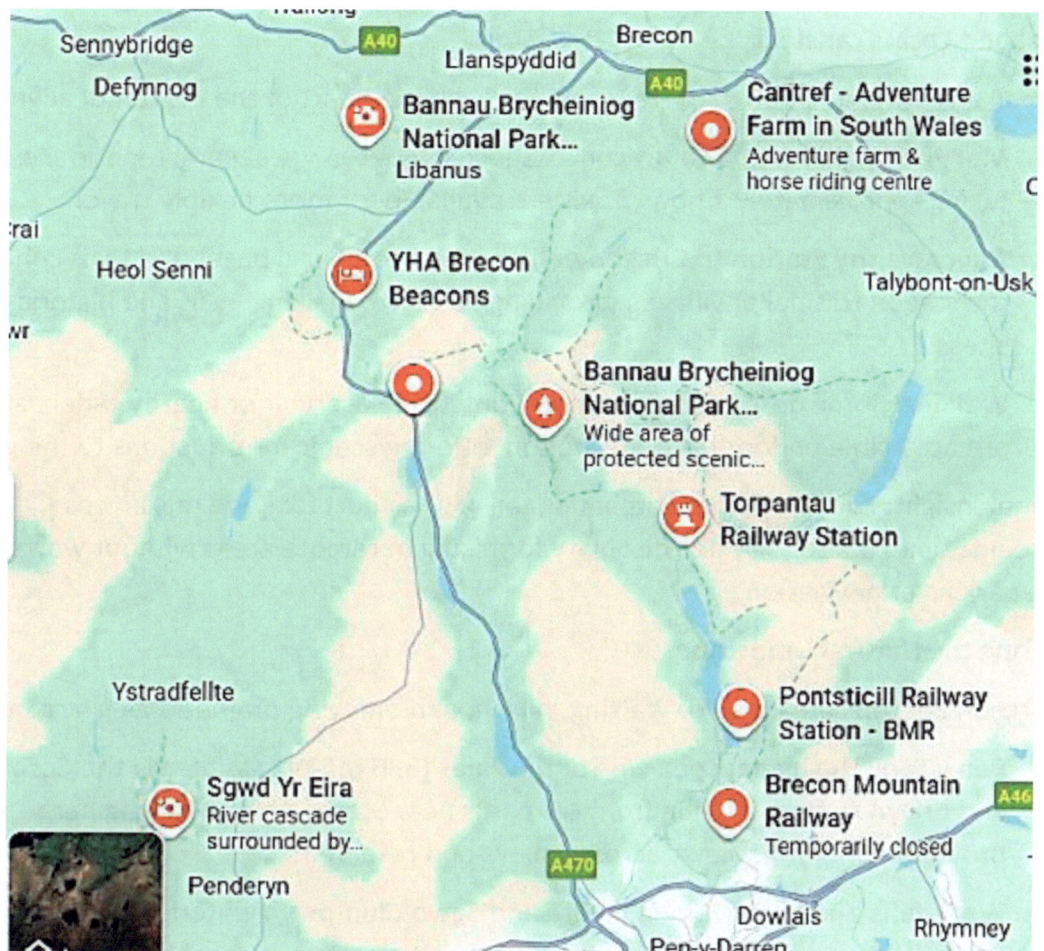

The Brecon Beacons trail route

- **From Cardiff:** Trains run from Cardiff Central to Merthyr Tydfil (45–50 minutes). From Merthyr, local buses or taxis provide access to the central Beacons and towns like Brecon.

- **From Swansea:** Trains to Neath or Pontardawe connect with bus services into the park.

- **From Hereford or Shrewsbury:** Services into Abergavenny or Crickhowell allow access to the northern Beacons.

Rail Tips: Booking in advance on Transport for Wales trains ensures reserved seating, particularly in summer when hikers and tourists fill the carriages. The journey from Cardiff offers striking views of valleys, rivers, and hillside villages.

Arrival and Local Transfers

Most rail arrivals require onward transport to reach the heart of the Brecon Beacons:

- **Merthyr Tydfil Station to Brecon:** Stagecoach buses run several times daily, taking approximately 1 hour. Taxis are available for more flexible travel.

- **Abergavenny Station to Crickhowell or Tretower:** Local buses and taxis connect the station to smaller villages, providing access to walking trails and historic sites.

- **Walking:** Some destinations, such as Pontsticill Reservoir or nearby canal paths, are accessible on foot from the station, offering scenic introductions to the park.

Personal Insight: I've found that combining rail with a short taxi ride maximizes sightseeing time. It also provides flexibility for hiking in remote areas without worrying about parking or navigation.

Exploring the Natural Landscapes

The Brecon Beacons are ideal for walking, hiking, and enjoying dramatic Welsh scenery:

- **Pen y Fan:** The highest peak in South Wales (886 m). Accessible via the Corn Du and Cribyn routes, starting from car parks near Storey Arms. Walking here provides panoramic views across valleys and reservoirs.

- **Waterfalls and Rivers:** Sgwd yr Eira and Sgwd Clun-gwyn waterfalls in the Waterfall Country near Pontneddfechan are accessible by local bus and offer short walks suitable for all levels.

- **Reservoirs and Lakes:** Pontsticill and Talybont Reservoirs are excellent for gentle walks or picnics, with surrounding trails offering peaceful riverside or forest views.

Travel Insight: Weather changes quickly in the Brecon Beacons. Early mornings often offer the clearest views, and bringing waterproof clothing is essential even in summer.

Historic Towns and Villages

The region's market towns provide cultural context and a chance to rest between walks:

- **Brecon:** Central hub with cathedral, canal, and Georgian architecture. Pubs such as The Royal Oak offer local ales, hearty meals, and insight into Welsh hospitality. Canal walks are ideal for casual strolls.

- **Crickhowell:** Picturesque village with stone bridge, independent shops, and cafés serving local cakes and coffee. Nearby Tretower Court and Castle highlight medieval history.
- **Abergavenny:** Known as the "Gateway to Wales," the town has a thriving food scene, including the popular Abergavenny Food Festival in September, plus historic sites such as the Abergavenny Castle ruins.

Personal Insight: Spending a night in Crickhowell or Brecon provides access to sunset and sunrise views over the hills, making photography and quiet exploration possible before the day-trippers arrive.

WALKING AND OUTDOOR ADVENTURES

Walking is central to experiencing the Brecon Beacons:

- **Short Walks:** Easy trails from Brecon town center along the Monmouthshire & Brecon Canal or around local reservoirs provide scenic highlights without full-day commitment.
- **Moderate Hikes:** Storey Arms to Pen y Fan is a popular day hike. Sgwd yr Eira Waterfall Walk is ideal for families and offers a chance to walk behind the waterfall.
- **Longer Treks:** The Beacons Way stretches 99 miles across the park, passing mountains, forests, and small villages, and is accessible in sections from various train and bus connections.

Travel Tip: Walking poles and sturdy boots are recommended, particularly for steep or muddy trails. Maps are available at Brecon visitor centers or online via the National Park Authority.

Food and Local Cuisine

The Brecon Beacons combine traditional Welsh cuisine with contemporary local dining:

- **Pubs and Inns:** Try lamb cawl (a traditional Welsh stew) or locally sourced beef in Brecon, Crickhowell, or Abergavenny. Local ales, including Taff Ale and Breconshire brews, are widely available.
- **Cafés:** Town cafés and village bakeries offer scones, cakes, and light lunches. Pontsticill and Talybont Reservoir areas have cafés catering to hikers.

- **Farm Shops:** Local cheese, meat, and preserves are sold in markets and small shops throughout the region, ideal for picnic lunches during walks.

Personal Insight: A picnic overlooking Pontsticill Reservoir with local cheese and oatcakes is one of my favorite ways to experience the Brecon Beacons. It allows time to absorb the scenery without rushing.

Seasonal Highlights

The experience of the Brecon Beacons varies with the seasons:

- **Spring (March–May):** Wildflowers bloom and rivers swell, ideal for waterfall walks and hillside hikes.
- **Summer (June–August):** Longer days allow for extended treks and early evening walks. Bus services to remote areas increase.
- **Autumn (September–November):** Golden foliage, crisp air, and quieter trails make photography particularly rewarding.
- **Winter (December–February):** Snow-dusted peaks create dramatic scenery, though trails may be icy. Shorter daylight requires careful planning for hikes.

Travel Insight: Visiting in spring or autumn balances mild weather, fewer tourists, and the best scenery for photography and wildlife spotting.

Cultural and Historic Highlights

The Brecon Beacons region has a rich heritage:

- **Brecon Cathedral:** Located in the town center, it offers historic architecture and occasional concerts.
- **Tretower Court and Castle:** Near Crickhowell, this medieval manor provides insight into Welsh history and feudal life.
- **Industrial Heritage:** Explore remnants of coal and iron industries near Merthyr Tydfil, with visitor centers detailing local history.

Personal Insight: Combining walks with historic sites enriches the hiking experience, linking natural beauty with cultural context.

Practical Map for Rail Travelers

- **Step 1:** Train to Merthyr Tydfil or Abergavenny from Cardiff or other cities.

- **Step 2:** Bus or taxi to Brecon, Crickhowell, or Tretower for walking, sightseeing, and local dining.
- **Step 3:** Short walks along canal paths, reservoirs, or Waterfall Country trails. Optional moderate hike to Pen y Fan from Storey Arms or local shuttle points.
- **Step 4:** Optional overnight stay in Brecon, Crickhowell, or Abergavenny for early morning hikes or photography.
- **Step 5:** Return to station for onward rail travel to Cardiff, Swansea, or Hereford.

This approach ensures flexibility, scenic enjoyment, and efficient use of public transport while prioritizing walking and exploration.

Exploring the Brecon Beacons by train and foot combines the best of Welsh landscapes, historic towns, and outdoor adventure. Rail travel minimizes driving while maximizing scenic enjoyment, and local buses, taxis, and walking trails connect visitors to valleys, waterfalls, and peaks. Balancing hiking, village exploration, and cultural experiences ensures a complete visit, whether for a day trip or multi-day adventure. The Brecon Beacons offer a mix of natural grandeur, historic charm, and local hospitality, making them a must-visit for anyone traveling through Wales by train.

CARDIFF TO PEMBROKESHIRE: A COASTAL ESCAPE

South Wales combines vibrant urban centers, rolling valleys, and a rugged coastline rich in history and natural beauty. A rail journey from Cardiff to Pembrokeshire offers an ideal mix of city culture and coastal serenity. This guide provides practical advice on train routes, local transfers, walking, culinary experiences, seasonal tips, and regional highlights to help travelers make the most of this scenic Welsh escape.

Planning the Journey

Train Routes

- **Cardiff to Pembroke Dock:** Great Western Railway (GWR) operates the route via Swansea and Carmarthen, continuing to Pembroke Dock.
- **Duration:** Approximately 3 hours 30 minutes from Cardiff Central to Pembroke Dock.
- **Frequency:** Several trains daily, with connections in Swansea or Carmarthen.

- **Scenic Insight:** The journey offers views of the Gower Peninsula near Swansea, the wide estuaries along Carmarthenshire, and the rolling hills of Pembrokeshire.

Cardiff to Pembrokeshire trail route

Tickets and Travel Tips

- **Advance Booking:** Recommended for weekends and summer to secure seats.
- **Off-Peak Travel:** Trains are quieter mid-morning or early afternoon.
- **First Class:** Offers more comfortable seating and tables, which is convenient for longer journeys and scenic observation.

Morning: Departing Cardiff

Cardiff Central Station

- Cardiff Central is modern and well-equipped, with cafes, shops, and luggage storage.
- **Breakfast Options:** Try **The Plan Café** or **The Potted Pig** for a hearty Welsh breakfast with locally sourced ingredients.
- **Sightseeing Before Departure:** If time allows, stroll from the station to Cardiff Castle or the Victorian Arcades for a quick taste of city culture.

First Leg: Cardiff to Swansea

- Trains leave Cardiff heading west through the Valleys and coastal plains.
- **Scenic Views:** On the left side, watch the Bristol Channel and coastal wetlands near Barry and Bridgend.
- Personal Insight: Early morning light highlights the patchwork fields and gentle estuaries, perfect for photography.

Mid-Morning: Swansea and the Gower Peninsula

Swansea Station

- Swansea is a compact city with riverside walks and nearby beaches.
- **Transfer Options:** From Swansea, local buses or taxis provide access to the Gower Peninsula, known for its dramatic cliffs and sandy beaches.
- Recommended stops: **Rhossili Bay** (15 miles by bus, 45-minute drive), **Three Cliffs Bay**, and **Oxwich Bay**.

Walking and Exploration

- Coastal paths are well-marked. Short walks along cliff-top trails offer panoramic views, and sandy beaches provide options for gentle strolls or picnics.
- Seasonal Tip: Spring and early summer showcase wildflowers along the cliffs; autumn brings quieter paths and golden light over the bay.

Lunch

- Coastal cafés in Gower serve fresh seafood, including mussels, crab, and locally caught fish. **The Worm's Head Hotel** at Rhossili is ideal for a seafood lunch overlooking the cliffs.
- Personal Insight: A packed picnic on the beach is equally rewarding—combine local cheese, bread, and cider for a simple yet memorable meal.

Afternoon: Carmarthenshire and Pembrokeshire Coast

Carmarthen Stop

- The train continues through Carmarthenshire, passing through scenic countryside with rolling hills, rivers, and farmland.

- Carmarthen Station is small but within walking distance of the town center, where you can explore traditional streets, historic churches, and local shops.
- Quick Walk Insight: A 10-minute stroll from the station leads to the medieval Carmarthen Bridge and riverside paths along the River Towy.

Pembrokeshire Arrival

- The final leg to Pembroke Dock passes through Milford Haven and Haverfordwest. Expect views of tidal estuaries, forests, and farmland.
- **Haverfordwest Station:** Central for exploring the county, including Haverfordwest Castle and the Riverside Walk.
- **Pembroke Dock Station:** Ideal for visiting Pembroke town, Pembroke Castle, and the start of coastal walks.

Evening: Pembrokeshire Villages and Coastal Walks

Pembroke

- Walk from the station to **Pembroke Castle**, a restored Norman castle surrounded by charming streets with pubs and cafés.
- Coastal walks along the **Cleddau Estuary** are accessible on foot or by short taxi rides.
- Seasonal Tip: Summer evenings are long and perfect for cliff-top walks; winter brings dramatic sunsets and fewer tourists.

Coastal Villages

- **Tenby:** Accessible by train from Pembroke Dock (10 minutes). Known for pastel-painted houses, sandy beaches, and medieval town walls.
- **Saundersfoot:** A small harbor village ideal for a gentle stroll, with cafés serving fish and chips or local cream teas.
- Personal Insight: Visit early morning or late afternoon for quieter streets and optimal light for photography.

Food and Drink Highlights

- **Seafood:** Fresh fish, lobster, crab, and scallops are widely available, often sourced from local harbors.

- **Local Specialties:** Welsh lamb, bara brith (fruit bread), and cawl (lamb or beef stew) are seasonal favorites.
- **Pubs and Cafés:** Many villages feature small pubs with locally brewed ales or cider; stop at **The Dolphin in Tenby** or **The Moorings at Saundersfoot** for waterfront dining.
- Tip: Try afternoon tea with scones and clotted cream in a village tearoom for a traditional Welsh experience.

Walking and Exploration Tips

- Pembrokeshire Coast Path offers short sections suitable for day walkers, with clear signage and maps available at visitor centers.
- Wear sturdy walking shoes; paths may be uneven, especially on cliff sections.
- Pack water, snacks, and layered clothing—the weather can change quickly along the coast.
- Combine walking with local buses or taxis to access more remote beaches or scenic points without long hikes.

Cultural Highlights Along the Route

- **Historic Castles:** Pembroke Castle, Carew Castle, and Haverfordwest Castle provide insights into the region's medieval history.
- **Museums and Heritage Centers:** Tenby Museum, Pembroke Dock Heritage Centre, and local craft centers showcase Welsh culture, maritime history, and local artisan products.
- **Festivals:** Summer events such as Tenby Arts Festival or Pembrokeshire Fish Week provide cultural immersion and seasonal flavors.

Seasonal Travel Tips

- **Spring:** Ideal for wildflower walks and mild weather; fewer tourists make coastal exploration more pleasant.
- **Summer:** Long days allow extended beach walks and village exploration, but book trains and accommodation early.
- **Autumn:** Golden light over beaches and cliffs enhances photography; seasonal seafood and game dishes appear on menus.

- **Winter:** Coastal walks are quieter and atmospheric; pack waterproof layers and warm clothing.

Practical Travel Advice

- **Transfers:** Taxis and local buses connect stations to beaches, villages, and scenic viewpoints. Check timetables, as services may be limited outside peak season.
- **Walking:** Most villages are compact; walking is the best way to explore harbors, town centers, and nearby beaches.
- **Connectivity:** Mobile signal may be patchy in rural areas; download maps and train/bus schedules in advance.
- **Luggage:** For day trips, bring a light daypack with water, snacks, camera, and weather-appropriate clothing.

Slow Travel Experience

Traveling from Cardiff to Pembrokeshire by train emphasizes enjoying the journey as much as the destination. Rolling farmland, tidal estuaries, and coastal cliffs unfold gradually, offering ample opportunities for observation, photography, and spontaneous stops.

- Spend time in coastal villages exploring shops, harbors, and beaches.
- Take advantage of slow walks along cliff paths or riverside trails to absorb local culture and scenery.
- Seasonal cuisine, including fresh seafood and traditional Welsh dishes, enhances the connection to place and makes meals part of the experience rather than just sustenance.

By combining rail travel, local transfers, and on-foot exploration, this journey balances comfort, discovery, and immersive coastal experiences.

A train journey from Cardiff to Pembrokeshire blends city culture with tranquil coastal scenery. Start in Cardiff for a cultural and culinary warm-up, then traverse Swansea and Carmarthenshire en route to Pembrokeshire. Explore castles, harbors, beaches, and cliff-top walks in villages like Pembroke, Tenby, and Saundersfoot. Seasonal planning, practical transfers, and a focus on slow travel allow visitors to fully appreciate South Wales' coastline, heritage, and food. This route is ideal for travelers seeking a scenic, relaxed, and culturally rich rail escape.

CHAPTER 7
THE GREAT WESTERN ROUTE: BRISTOL TO CORNWALL

The Great Western Route is one of Britain's most iconic rail journeys, stretching from the vibrant city of Bristol to the rugged, dramatic landscapes of Cornwall. This route offers not only a comfortable and efficient way to explore one of the most picturesque regions of the UK, but also an unforgettable opportunity to witness stunning coastal views, historical landmarks, and charming towns. Whether you're a first-time visitor or a seasoned traveler, this journey is a must-do for anyone eager to experience the true beauty of the West of England.

Bristol To Cornwall scenic route

GETTING STARTED: THE DEPARTURE FROM BRISTOL

Bristol, a lively city known for its maritime history and vibrant arts scene, is the perfect starting point for this rail adventure. The main station, Bristol Temple Meads, is a historic Victorian-era building that serves as the gateway to the West Country. It is well-connected to major cities across the UK, making it a convenient departure point.

Before embarking on your journey, consider spending some time in Bristol. Explore the city's harborside, visit the famous Clifton Suspension Bridge for panoramic views, or wander through the independent shops and cafes of Stokes Croft. For lunch or a coffee break, head to **St. Nicholas Market** for local delicacies such as a **Cornish pasty** or a **Bristol cream tea**.

Once on board the train, you'll begin your journey westward toward Cornwall. The train travels along the **Great Western Railway (GWR)**, operated by Great Western Railway, and offers a range of ticket options, including standard and first-class seating. Trains on this route are modern and comfortable, with onboard services like free Wi-Fi, power sockets, and refreshments, making it easy to relax and enjoy the ride.

The Journey: From Bristol to Exeter

As the train leaves Bristol, you'll start to notice the change in landscape. The first leg of your journey takes you through the rolling hills of **Somerset** and **Devon**. The route is known for its natural beauty, offering glimpses of the countryside and the beginnings of the Devon coastline.

One of the highlights along this stretch is the town of **Taunton**, known for its historical significance and its proximity to the stunning **Quantock Hills**. While the train doesn't stop here, it's worth noting that Taunton is a short detour if you wish to explore the area. You can easily reach Taunton via local buses or trains for a hiking opportunity in the hills or a visit to the 12th-century **Taunton Castle**.

As you approach Exeter, the scene becomes even more captivating, with the **Exe River** winding through the landscape. Exeter itself is a delightful stop, with its medieval **Exeter Cathedral** and charming **underground passages** that date back to Roman times. If you have time to spare, the city is known for its historic pubs, such as **The Old Firehouse**, famous for its hearty pies and local ales.

Exeter to Plymouth: Coastal Beauty

The next stretch of the journey takes you along the coast, with views of **Devon's** dramatic cliffs and the sparkling sea in the distance. This is a truly scenic part of the route, where the train hugs the coastline and offers passengers a glimpse of what is to come as you move further south.

Exeter to Plymouth scenic coastal charm

Plymouth, a historic naval city, is a key stop on the Great Western Route. The train station here is just a short walk from the **Plymouth Hoe**, a large public space that offers breathtaking views of the English Channel. If you're a fan of maritime history, a visit to the **Mayflower Steps** is essential — this is the spot from which the Pilgrims famously set sail for America in 1620.

For those looking to experience the best of Devon's coast, consider a detour to the nearby **Dartmoor National Park**, accessible by a short local transfer from Plymouth. Dartmoor is known for its granite tors, wild ponies, and numerous walking trails. It's an ideal place for a bit of outdoor adventure before continuing your rail journey south.

Plymouth to Truro: The Heart of Cornwall

As the train continues its journey from Plymouth toward Truro, you begin to feel the essence of Cornwall's charm. The route takes you through lush, verdant landscapes dotted with ancient stone circles and quaint villages. This section of the journey offers incredible views, especially as you approach the town of **St. Austell**.

St. Austell is home to the world-famous **Eden Project**, an environmental wonder and one of Cornwall's top attractions. The Eden Project is easily accessible by local bus or taxi from the St. Austell train station, and it offers visitors a chance to walk through massive biomes housing tropical and Mediterranean plants. Whether you have a few hours or a full day, the Eden Project is a must-see.

Your final destination on this stretch is **Truro**, Cornwall's cathedral city. Truro is the cultural and shopping hub of Cornwall, and it is home to the magnificent **Truro Cathedral**, with its stunning gothic architecture. Take time to wander through the cobbled streets of the city, exploring local boutiques, and sampling Cornish delicacies like **Cornish cream teas** or **Cornish ice cream**. If you're a fan of history, be sure to check out **Royal Cornwall Museum**, which showcases the region's rich heritage.

Truro to Falmouth: A Glimpse of Cornwall's Coastline

If you're continuing your journey further into Cornwall, the next stop is **Falmouth**, a charming coastal town located at the end of the rail line. To reach Falmouth from Truro, it's a short but scenic journey along the **Falmouth Branch Line**. The route offers stunning coastal views and takes you through picturesque Cornish countryside before arriving in this vibrant seaside town.

Falmouth is home to **Pendennis Castle**, one of the best-preserved coastal artillery forts in England, which offers dramatic views across the bay. Additionally, Falmouth's **National Maritime Museum** provides an in-depth look at the region's long naval history, while the **Gyllyngvase Beach** offers a tranquil spot to relax by the sea.

Practical Tips for the Journey

- **Travel Time**: The entire journey from Bristol to Cornwall takes approximately 4-5 hours by train, depending on the route and stops.
- **Best Time to Travel**: The Great Western Route is beautiful year-round, but spring and summer offer the best weather for enjoying coastal views and outdoor activities. Autumn also offers the advantage of fewer tourists, with beautiful fall foliage along the route.
- **Tickets and Passes**: For savings, consider purchasing a **BritRail Pass**, which provides unlimited travel on the UK's national rail network. Alternatively,

- booking tickets in advance through **Great Western Railway's website** can often yield discounts.
- **Luggage**: For those planning to hike or explore the region, it's advisable to travel light. Many stations offer luggage storage, and many local buses and ferries allow larger backpacks or day bags.

The Great Western Route is a perfect blend of scenic beauty, historical charm, and modern convenience. It's an excellent way to explore the diversity of the West Country, offering something for everyone — from urban excitement in Bristol to the coastal serenity of Cornwall. Whether you're a history buff, nature lover, or culture seeker, this journey will leave you with lasting memories of one of Britain's most beautiful regions.

Remember to take the time to step off the train at key stations, explore the towns and villages, and discover the hidden gems that make this route so special. The journey itself is as rewarding as the destinations.

BRISTOL: THE CULTURAL GATEWAY TO THE WEST

Bristol, in southwest England, is a vibrant city that combines rich maritime history, street art, and a dynamic cultural scene. Well-connected by rail, it serves as the gateway to the West Country, including Bath, the Cotswolds, and the scenic Mendip Hills. Whether arriving for a day trip or as a base for exploring southwest England, Bristol's train stations provide convenient access to historic districts, waterfront attractions, and the surrounding countryside.

GETTING TO BRISTOL BY TRAIN

Bristol Temple Meads is the city's main station, offering direct services from London Paddington, Birmingham, Cardiff, and Exeter. High-speed and regional services make it an ideal hub for West Country exploration.

- **London to Bristol:** Great Western Railway offers frequent direct services taking approximately **1 hour 45 minutes**.
- **Cardiff to Bristol:** Cross-country trains connect in around **50 minutes**, passing through scenic Severn Estuary views.
- **Bristol Parkway:** Located north of the city center, ideal for travelers connecting from the Midlands or heading west toward Bath and the Cotswolds.

Practical Tips:

- Temple Meads is central and within walking distance of the historic city center.
- Early booking can secure cheaper tickets on long-distance services.
- Temple Meads and Parkway both have luggage facilities and accessible platforms.

Temple Meads and the Waterfront

Temple Meads Station itself is a historic landmark, designed by Isambard Kingdom Brunel. Its Victorian architecture sets the tone for a city steeped in history.

- **Bristol Harbour:** A short 10–15-minute walk from the station, this regenerated waterfront combines historic ships, museums, and cafes.
- **SS Great Britain:** Brunel's iconic steamship and museum are easily accessible on foot from the harbor.
- **M Shed Museum:** Focuses on Bristol's social and industrial history, ideal for a 1–2-hour visit.

Food & Drink:

- **The Cornubia:** A waterfront pub offering seafood platters and local ales.
- **Watershed Café:** Overlooking the harbor, serves light meals, coffee, and cakes with riverside views.

Seasonal Tips: Spring and summer are best for outdoor seating and harbor walks; autumn and winter bring quieter streets and atmospheric fogs over the docks.

HISTORIC CITY CENTER AND CULTURAL HIGHLIGHTS

Bristol's city center is compact and walkable from Temple Meads. Key cultural and historic sites include:

- **Bristol Cathedral:** Magnificent Gothic architecture with gardens and cloisters.
- **St Nicholas Market:** A bustling indoor market with international street food, artisan crafts, and local produce.
- **Broadmead and Cabot Circus:** For modern shopping, cafes, and entertainment.

Street Art and Graffiti: Bristol is the birthplace of **Banksy**, and guided walking tours reveal murals and hidden street art across neighborhoods like Stokes Croft.

Cultural Tip: Weekdays are less crowded for museums and markets; weekends offer more local events but can be busy.

Neighborhoods and Local Walks

- **Clifton:** Accessible by a 15–20-minute bus or a 30-minute walk from the city center. Explore **Clifton Suspension Bridge**, parklands, and boutique shops.
- **Redland & Cotham:** Tree-lined streets with Georgian architecture, ideal for a quiet stroll.
- **Bristol Harbourside Walks:** A 1–2-hour route along the floating harbor and historic quays, passing pubs, galleries, and small cafes.

Food & Drink Recommendations:

- **The Cowshed:** Renowned for locally sourced steaks and small plates.
- **Boston Tea Party:** Chain café serving brunch, coffee, and vegetarian-friendly meals.

Personal Insight: Walking from Temple Meads through the city center to Clifton offers a mix of industrial heritage, modern culture, and panoramic views over the Avon Gorge.

Day Trips from Bristol by Train

Bristol is perfectly positioned for rail day trips across the West Country:

- **Bath:** Frequent services via Bristol Temple Meads to **Bath Spa**, 12–15 minutes by train. Explore Roman Baths, Georgian crescents, and boutique shopping.
- **Weston-super-Mare:** Coastal town with sandy beaches, a 45-minute ride via Great Western Railway. Enjoy promenade walks and traditional seaside activities.
- **Cheddar Gorge & Mendip Hills:** Access via Bristol Parkway and local buses. Ideal for hiking, caving, and scenic photography.

Rail Tips: Many rural and coastal destinations require checking bus or taxi connections from stations; combining train and foot travel is often the most scenic and practical approach.

Seasonal and Cultural Events

- **Upfest:** Europe's largest street art festival, held in July, showcasing murals, live art, and workshops.
- **Bristol Harbour Festival:** Late July, celebrates maritime history with music, food, and tall ships.
- **Christmas Market:** November–December, offers seasonal crafts, food, and drinks at the city center.

Seasonal Insight: Spring and summer offer long daylight for city walks and harbor exploration. Autumn provides rich colors across parks and gardens, while winter is ideal for museum visits and festive events.

Local Cuisine and Dining Experiences

Bristol's culinary scene is diverse, focusing on local, sustainable ingredients:

- **Seafood:** The waterfront offers fresh catches, including mackerel, crab, and mussels.
- **Bristol Cream Teas:** Try at cafes such as **Boston Tea Party** or small independent tearooms.
- **Vegan & Vegetarian:** Bristol is highly vegetarian-friendly, with multiple plant-based restaurants like **Root** in Stokes Croft.

Personal Insight: Sampling street food at St Nicholas Market and following it with a walk along the harborside provides a full culinary and cultural experience without moving far from the train station.

Practical Travel Tips

- **Tickets:** Off-peak travel from London or Cardiff is cheaper, with options to book via Great Western Railway or National Rail.
- **Walking Routes:** Most cultural and historic attractions are within 20–30 minutes' walk from Temple Meads.
- **Transfers:** Use local buses for neighborhoods like Clifton or the Downs. Taxis are readily available from the station.
- **Weather:** South-west England can be wet; carry waterproofs when walking between districts.

Photography & Scenic Notes: The best views are from the harbor, Clifton Suspension Bridge, and from the city center across the Avon Gorge. Sunrise and late afternoon light add drama to the historic architecture.

Personal Insight

Bristol combines heritage and modernity seamlessly. Arriving by train, you are immediately immersed in Victorian architecture at Temple Meads, then swept into vibrant harbor scenes and colorful street art within minutes. Walking to Clifton provides dramatic views over the Avon Gorge, and nearby day trips expand the experience into Roman history, seaside leisure, and rural charm. I recommend setting aside a full day for the city and another for rail-connected excursions to fully experience the West Country's diversity.

Tip: Start early at Temple Meads, walk the harbor and city center, have lunch at a local café, then take a bus or short train to Clifton or a nearby village for the afternoon.

Bristol is more than a city; it is the **cultural gateway to the West**, blending historic architecture, maritime heritage, modern art, and culinary innovation. Rail access makes it a practical hub for exploring both the city and the wider region, from Bath and the Cotswolds to coastal towns and the Mendip Hills. Seasonal events, museums, local food, and accessible walking routes make Bristol a memorable first stop for any journey through southwest England.

Whether your focus is history, culture, or the outdoors, traveling to and from Bristol by train offers convenience, comfort, and immersion in the West Country's best experiences—all within easy reach of the station.

DISCOVERING CORNWALL'S COASTLINE AND HIDDEN CORNERS

Cornwall, the southwestern tip of England, is a landscape of rugged cliffs, golden beaches, fishing villages, and charming market towns. Exploring Cornwall by train offers a relaxed and scenic approach to this region, allowing visitors to enjoy the dramatic coastline and discover hidden corners without the stress of driving narrow country lanes. This guide focuses on routes, experiences, culture, food, seasonal highlights, and practical travel tips for rail travelers.

Cornwall, the southwestern tip of England

GETTING TO CORNWALL BY TRAIN

Cornwall is accessible via mainline services from London and other English cities:

- **London Paddington to Penzance:** Great Western Railway (GWR) operates direct trains taking approximately 5 hours, with comfortable seating, free Wi-Fi, and panoramic views of Devon and Cornwall.

- **Bristol, Exeter, and Plymouth:** Regional services connect via Penzance or St Ives. Changing at Plymouth provides access to the Looe Valley and Tamar Valley lines.

- **Scenic Lines Within Cornwall:** The St Ives Bay Line (St Erth to St Ives) and the Atlantic Coast Line (Par to Newquay) offer short yet breathtaking journeys through coastal scenery.

Travel Insight: For panoramic views, request a seat on the left side northbound or westbound trains from Exeter toward Penzance. Early morning departures provide calm, clear light for photography.

Arrival and Local Transfers

Rail travel in Cornwall is complemented by buses, taxis, ferries, and walking paths to reach the region's hidden gems:

- **Penzance Station:** Central and convenient, with taxi services to St Michael's Mount or nearby coastal villages. Bus connections link to Mousehole, Marazion, and Land's End.

- **St Erth Station:** Gateway to St Ives via the St Ives Bay Line. The 15–20-minute train ride offers coastal views.

- **Par Station:** Connects with the Par to Newquay branch line, ideal for exploring the north coast beaches and surf towns.

Personal Insight: Cornwall's rail stations are generally small but strategically located, making it easy to combine train travel with walking and short bus trips. A combination of rail and foot travel is often faster than driving in summer traffic.

EXPLORING COASTAL SCENERY

Cornwall's coastline is its defining feature, with dramatic cliffs, secluded coves, and sandy beaches accessible by rail and foot:

- **St Ives:** Accessible from St Erth, St Ives is famous for its beaches, art galleries (Tate St Ives), and narrow streets. The coastal walk to Carbis Bay offers stunning views.

- **Porthcurno and Minack Theatre:** Take a bus or taxi from Penzance to Porthcurno. The open-air Minack Theatre, perched on cliffs above the Atlantic, is a must-see. The adjacent Porthcurno Beach is ideal for a short walk or picnic.

- **Looe and Polperro:** The Looe Valley Line from Liskeard takes you to Looe, with historic harbors and sandy beaches. Walking trails along the coast or to Polperro reveal hidden coves and fishing villages.

- **Land's End:** Accessible via bus from Penzance or St Ives, Land's End is the southwesternmost point of Britain with panoramic cliff views. Combine with nearby Sennen Cove for a coastal hike.

Travel Insight: The St Ives Bay Line is particularly scenic, hugging the coastline with glimpses of turquoise water and sandy beaches. Bring binoculars for seabird spotting along cliffs.

Hidden Cornish Villages and Market Towns

Cornwall's villages and towns offer culture, history, and local charm:

- **Mousehole:** A short bus ride from Penzance, this fishing village features narrow streets, stone cottages, and art galleries. Evening walks along the harbor are especially atmospheric.

- **Marazion:** Home to St Michael's Mount, accessible by foot via a causeway at low tide or by boat. The medieval castle and gardens are a highlight.

- **Fowey:** Accessible via Par or Bodmin Parkway with a short ferry or bus ride. Explore historic streets, waterfront pubs, and literary heritage (Daphne du Maurier connections).

- **Truro:** Cornwall's cathedral city is reachable by train from Penzance and serves as a hub for exploring nearby attractions. Georgian architecture, markets, and shopping are highlights.

Personal Insight: Many hidden corners, such as Cadgwith Cove or Mullion, are best accessed via a combination of train and bus. Planning connections in advance ensures maximum exploration time.

WALKING AND OUTDOOR ACTIVITIES

Walking and coastal exploration are central to a Cornish itinerary:

- **South West Coast Path:** Sections are accessible from St Ives, Penzance, and Fowey. Even short walks provide dramatic cliff-top views.

- **Beach Walks:** Porthminster, Porthcurno, and Polzeath offer sandy stretches for gentle walking or paddling.

- **Water-Based Activities:** Surfing, kayaking, or paddleboarding are available at Newquay and Fistral Beach, reachable via the Atlantic Coast Line.

Travel Tip: Many coastal paths are steep or uneven; good walking shoes and layers are essential. Summer brings busy beaches, so early morning walks are recommended.

Food and Local Cuisine

Cornwall is famous for seafood, cream teas, and artisanal produce:

- **Seafood:** Fresh crab, lobster, and Cornish mackerel are widely available at harborside restaurants in St Ives, Looe, and Fowey.

- **Cornish Pasty:** Served across towns and villages, often from small bakeries near stations. Try traditional beef and potato or explore local variations.

- **Cream Tea:** Afternoon tea with scones, clotted cream, and jam is a Cornish classic. Penzance, St Ives, and Fowey cafés excel at this.
- **Markets:** Truro and St Ives host weekly markets with local cheeses, meats, and vegetables, perfect for a picnic while exploring.

Personal Insight: A Cornish pasty on the St Ives Bay Line train makes a memorable, scenic snack—combine with a window seat for ocean views.

Seasonal Highlights

Cornwall's experience varies by season:

- **Spring (March–May):** Wildflowers bloom along cliffs, seas are calmer, and coastal walks are quieter.
- **Summer (June–August):** Long days, warm beaches, and vibrant festivals. Trains and towns are busy—book tickets in advance.
- **Autumn (September–November):** Golden sunsets and fewer crowds create ideal photography conditions.
- **Winter (December–February):** Dramatic storms on the coast create powerful scenery, though some ferries or outdoor attractions may close.

Travel Insight: Spring and autumn offer the best combination of mild weather, fewer tourists, and outstanding coastal lighting for photography.

Cultural and Historic Highlights

Cornwall's culture is intertwined with maritime history, mining heritage, and art:

- **Tate St Ives:** Modern and contemporary art with focus on Cornwall's artists.
- **Geevor Tin Mine:** Near Penzance, explore Cornwall's mining past, part of the UNESCO World Heritage mining landscape.
- **Maritime Heritage:** Lighthouses, harbors, and museums in Penzance and Falmouth highlight Cornwall's seafaring history.
- **Festivals:** St Ives September Festival, Falmouth Week, and local food festivals showcase arts, music, and culinary culture.

Personal Insight: Cornwall's hidden corners often reveal small museums, craft shops, and galleries tucked away in villages—a short walk from the station can uncover unique local experiences.

Practical Map for Rail Travelers

- **Step 1:** Train from London Paddington → Penzance (5h) or via Plymouth.
- **Step 2:** Local trains or buses to St Erth → St Ives for art, beaches, and coastal walks.
- **Step 3:** Bus or taxi from Penzance to Mousehole, Marazion, and Minack Theatre. Walk St Michael's Mount at low tide.
- **Step 4:** Atlantic Coast Line from Par → Newquay for beaches and water sports.
- **Step 5:** Optional side trips to Looe, Polperro, and Fowey via Liskeard or Bodmin Parkway.
- **Step 6:** Return to Penzance or Truro for onward travel.

This plan balances scenic rail journeys, hidden coastal corners, and walking access while maximizing flexibility and minimizing reliance on cars.

Discovering Cornwall by train is an immersive experience, combining scenic journeys, coastal exploration, historic towns, and local cuisine. Trains provide access to both popular destinations like St Ives and hidden corners like Mousehole and Porthcurno. By combining rail travel with local buses, taxis, and walking, travelers can experience Cornwall's dramatic coastline, beaches, and charming villages efficiently and comfortably. Planning for daylight travel, seasonal weather, and optional stopovers ensures a memorable Cornish adventure.

EXPLORING THE COASTAL RAILWAY BETWEEN DEVON AND CORNWALL

The railway line connecting Devon and Cornwall offers one of the most iconic coastal journeys in Britain. Stretching from Exeter in Devon to Penzance in Cornwall, the route passes rugged cliffs, sandy beaches, fishing villages, and rolling countryside. Traveling by train provides a unique perspective, combining the comfort of rail with access to coastal trails, historic towns, and regional culinary delights. This guide outlines the route, local transfers, walking options, seasonal tips, and practical advice for a full day—or longer—of exploration.

The railway line connecting Devon and Cornwall coastal trail

Planning the Journey

Train Routes

- **Operators:** Great Western Railway (GWR) operates the mainline service between Exeter St Davids and Penzance.

- **Duration:** Direct trains take around 4–4.5 hours. Local stopping services are slower but allow access to smaller coastal towns.

- **Scenic Highlights:** Views of the English Riviera near Dawlish, the Exe Estuary, and the dramatic cliffs of North Cornwall are among the route's defining features.

- **Frequency:** Trains run approximately every 30–60 minutes, with additional services in summer.

Tickets and Travel Tips

- **Advance Booking:** Recommended during summer and bank holidays; coastal routes are popular with tourists.

- **Seat Choice:** Sit on the left-hand side when heading west for better views of the coastline between Dawlish and St Ives.

- **First Class:** Offers larger seats, tables, and panoramic windows, perfect for photography and working or relaxing during long journeys.

Morning: Exeter to Dawlish and Teignmouth

Exeter St Davids Station

- Exeter St Davids is well-equipped with cafés, shops, and luggage storage.
- **Breakfast:** Local options include **The Station Café** or **Café 37** for coffee, pastries, or a traditional Cornish pasty before departure.

Dawlish

- **Travel Time:** Around 30 minutes from Exeter by train.
- Dawlish is known for its long sea wall and Black Head cliffs.
- **Walking Tip:** A gentle stroll along the sea wall provides excellent views of the English Channel and Dawlish Warren Nature Reserve.
- Seasonal Insight: Spring and summer bring colourful wildflowers along the cliffs, while winter storms offer dramatic coastal photography.

Teignmouth

- A short 10-minute train ride from Dawlish.
- Historic harbor town with sandy beaches and Victorian promenade.
- Recommended cafés: **The Black Prince Café** or **Steamer Coffee House** for light lunch or afternoon tea.

LATE MORNING: NEWTON ABBOT TO TORBAY

Torquay, Paignton, and Brixham

- The line curves along Torbay, offering panoramic views of the bay.
- **Torquay:** Walkable from the station to the harbor, beaches, and Italianate architecture. Visit **Torquay Museum** for regional history.
- **Paignton:** Known for its Victorian pier and beach. Local buses connect to the Paignton Zoo or South Devon Coastal Path.
- **Brixham:** Not directly on the main line; accessible via a short bus or taxi from Paignton. Famous for fishing harbor and seafood markets.
- Personal Insight: Early afternoon is ideal for a harbor walk and fresh seafood tasting. Crab sandwiches or Cornish sardines are seasonal highlights.

Afternoon: Crossing into Cornwall

Kingswear and Dartmouth

- Accessed via a branch line from Paignton or a local ferry across the River Dart.
- **Dartmouth:** Historic maritime town with castle views, narrow streets, and riverside walks. The ferry provides easy crossing for photography and coastal exploration.

Looe and Polperro (Optional Stops)

- For more remote villages, local trains from Plymouth or bus connections provide access to picturesque fishing villages.
- **Polperro:** Narrow cobbled streets, historic cottages, and a small harbor. Ideal for short walks, artisan shops, and cream teas.

Evening: St Ives, Penzance, and the Cornish Coast

St Ives

- **Access:** Change at St Erth from the main line.
- St Ives is a hub for art and culture, including the Tate St Ives and Barbara Hepworth Museum.
- Coastal walks around Porthmeor and Porthgwidden beaches offer excellent sunset views.
- **Dining:** Seafood is exceptional. Try **The Seafood Café** or **Porthminster Beach Café** for fresh catch and Cornish cream.

Penzance

- **Arrival:** Final stop on the mainline.
- Walkable from the station to the harbor, historic streets, and St Michael's Mount (reachable via causeway at low tide).
- Seasonal tip: Summer brings festivals, music, and outdoor markets; winter offers quiet streets and storm-watched cliffs.

Cultural and Scenic Highlights

- **Historic Towns:** Exeter Cathedral, Torquay Victorian promenade, Dartmouth maritime history, and St Ives art heritage.

- **Coastal Paths:** South West Coast Path runs along most of the line, allowing short or full-day walks with breathtaking views.
- **Wildlife:** Watch seabirds, seals, and occasionally dolphins along the coast; Dawlish Warren Nature Reserve is excellent for birdwatching.
- **Local Arts:** St Ives has galleries showcasing local artists, and Newlyn near Penzance features contemporary art and crafts.

Food and Drink Highlights

- **Seafood:** Crab, mackerel, scallops, and Cornish sardines are widely available along the route.
- **Cornish Specialties:** Cornish pasties, saffron buns, and clotted cream teas.
- **Pubs and Cafés:** From Dawlish to Penzance, coastal pubs serve local ales and seasonal dishes. Recommended stops: **The Black Lion in Dawlish**, **The Fisherman's Arms in Polperro**, and **The Shore Restaurant in St Ives**.

Seasonal Travel Tips

- **Spring:** Wildflowers, mild temperatures, and quieter trains. Ideal for walking coastal paths.
- **Summer:** Long days for extended exploration; book trains and accommodation early.
- **Autumn:** Golden light and fewer tourists make for peaceful travel. Seafood and seasonal produce are excellent.
- **Winter:** Dramatic coastline during storms; quieter villages. Check train services in advance for potential weather disruptions.

Practical Travel Advice

- **Transfers:** Use local buses or taxis to reach coastal villages not directly served by the mainline.
- **Walking:** Paths along cliffs and beaches are often uneven; wear sturdy footwear.
- **Luggage:** For day trips, a light daypack with water, snacks, and camera is sufficient.

- **Connectivity:** Signal may be patchy in remote coastal sections; download maps and train schedules in advance.

Slow Travel Experience

The Devon–Cornwall coastal railway encourages travelers to savor the journey as much as the destinations. Rolling countryside, dramatic cliffs, and historic harbors unfold gradually from the train window, allowing reflection, photography, and spontaneous exploration.

- Spend time in harbors, walking narrow streets, and sampling local cuisine.
- Combine rail travel with walking along cliff paths or short bus connections to hidden beaches.
- Seasonal seafood and traditional Cornish dishes add depth to the slow travel experience, letting you taste the region as well as see it.

This journey is ideal for those who appreciate scenic rail travel, coastal culture, and immersive exploration without the rush of a car-based itinerary.

The Devon–Cornwall coastal railway blends urban centers, fishing villages, and dramatic coastal scenery. Begin in Exeter, travel along the English Riviera, explore Dartmouth and remote Cornish villages, and finish in St Ives or Penzance. Seasonal planning, local transfers, and a focus on walking and slow exploration allow travelers to enjoy South West England fully. This route offers comfort, scenery, history, and culinary delights, making it a quintessential coastal rail experience.

CHAPTER 8
PRACTICAL TRAVEL TIPS FOR 2026 TRAIN EXPLORERS

Traveling by train in Britain offers one of the most scenic and convenient ways to explore the country. Whether you're embarking on a leisurely journey through the countryside, a quick hop to the next city, or a multi-day adventure across regions, understanding the ins and outs of rail travel can make your experience smoother and more enjoyable. In this section, we provide a set of essential tips to help you make the most of your 2026 rail journey, covering everything from ticketing to local transfers, seasonal advice, and insider knowledge.

CHOOSING THE RIGHT TICKET AND PASS

Before you even board your train, selecting the right ticket or rail pass can significantly impact your journey. Whether you're planning to travel across multiple regions or just taking a few short trips, knowing your options can save time and money.

- **Advance Tickets**: These are the most economical choice if you know your travel dates in advance. Prices can be much lower than flexible tickets, especially for long-distance journeys. Book early through the official **National Rail Enquiries** website or via train operators like **Great Western Railway** and **Avanti West Coast**.

- **Rail Passes**: For visitors, the **BritRail Pass** is a fantastic option. It offers unlimited travel across the UK's rail network for a set number of days. The pass can be used flexibly, allowing for multiple train journeys within a certain time frame. Another popular option is the **BritRail England Pass**, which covers all of England and offers discounts for groups or children. If you plan to travel extensively by train, this can be an excellent value.

- **Flexible Tickets**: If you prefer more flexibility, **off-peak** or **flexible tickets** allow you to travel on a wider range of trains. However, these tickets tend to be pricier than advance options, so they are best if you need the freedom to change your travel times or locations without penalties.

- **Seat Reservations**: For popular routes, such as London to Edinburgh or during busy travel seasons, seat reservations can be highly beneficial. These reservations guarantee you a spot, especially on fast intercity trains. While not mandatory on all trains, they are recommended during peak hours or holiday periods.

Train Travel Essentials: What to Pack and Expect

When traveling by train, comfort and preparation can make a big difference. Here are a few key tips to ensure you're well-prepared for your rail adventure:

- **Packing**: Pack light but smart. Large suitcases can be cumbersome on trains, especially during rush hour. Most trains offer luggage racks, but if you're traveling during busy periods, smaller bags are easier to manage. Consider packing a small day bag for essentials like snacks, a water bottle, maps, or a guidebook, especially on long journeys.

- **Electronics**: Many trains now offer free Wi-Fi and power sockets, especially on intercity services like **Avanti West Coast** and **Great Western Railway**. However, not all trains have reliable service, so bring a portable charger just in case. Having a downloaded map or itinerary can be useful for offline navigation.

- **Food and Drink**: While most trains offer a café or trolley service, it's always a good idea to bring your own snacks. British rail stations often have excellent food options, with many featuring local produce or regional specialties. Look out for **Cornish pasties** in stations near Cornwall, or **Yorkshire curd tarts** in the north. Many stations also have food courts with various choices if you're waiting for a train.

- **Comfort Items**: If you're traveling on longer journeys, bring a neck pillow, blanket, or even an eye mask for added comfort. Many trains, especially overnight ones, offer sleeper cabins with beds for longer trips, but if you're just riding for a few hours, being prepared will help you feel more comfortable.

NAVIGATING TRAIN STATIONS: ARRIVAL AND TRANSFERS

Train stations in Britain can range from massive, bustling hubs to charming, smaller platforms. Regardless of size, it's essential to be familiar with your departure and arrival locations.

- **Station Layouts**: Larger stations like **London King's Cross**, **Manchester Piccadilly**, and **Edinburgh Waverley** can be overwhelming, so it's helpful to know the station layout in advance. Look for signs or maps indicating platforms, ticket machines, and amenities. If you're unfamiliar with the station, it's always a good idea to arrive a little earlier to familiarize yourself with the surroundings.

- **Transfers and Connections**: For some routes, you may need to transfer between different stations or platforms. In major cities like London, you can easily transfer between different rail companies, as well as to the **London Underground** (subway). In cities like **Glasgow** and **Bristol**, buses, taxis, or even river ferries can provide alternative transfers if you need to reach more remote destinations.

- **Accessibility**: Britain's rail system is increasingly accessible for people with disabilities, but it's always worth checking in advance if you need assistance. Most train operators, including **Trainline** and **National Rail**, offer services like step-free access or assistance with boarding. Stations often have information desks, and it's recommended to give at least 24 hours' notice for special requirements.

Seasonal Considerations: When to Travel

The UK's weather can be unpredictable, so planning your train trip according to the season is key to making the most of your experience.

- **Spring and Summer (March to August)**: These months are ideal for exploring the British countryside by rail. Longer daylight hours offer plenty of time to enjoy the panoramic views. This is also the time when train services are most frequent, though it's important to book in advance during peak travel periods, such as **Easter**, **Bank Holidays**, and **summer school vacations**. Expect lush green landscapes, coastal views, and outdoor festivals in many cities.

- **Autumn (September to November)**: Fall is one of the most beautiful times to travel by rail, as the country is awash with autumnal colors. Many train routes pass through forests, mountains, and rolling hills, where the changing leaves provide a stunning backdrop. However, the weather can be cooler and wetter, so be sure to pack an umbrella and layers. Train tickets tend to be more affordable during this season as well.

- **Winter (December to February)**: Winter train travel is a peaceful, scenic experience, especially when heading toward mountainous regions like the **Scottish Highlands** or **the Lake District**. However, winter weather can cause delays, so it's advisable to check for any disruptions. Trains tend to be quieter, but if you're hoping for a cozy experience, some train services offer festive afternoon teas or winter-themed routes.

HIDDEN GEMS BY RAIL: REGIONAL HIGHLIGHTS TO EXPLORE

The UK rail network offers easy access to some of the country's lesser-known gems, providing travelers with a chance to explore more remote or off-the-beaten-path destinations.

- **The Cotswolds**: Accessible via **Great Western Railway**, this picturesque region of rolling hills, honey-colored stone villages, and medieval market towns is a must-see for those wanting a taste of quintessential English charm. Trains from London to **Moreton-in-Marsh** or **Kingham** offer direct access to the heart of the Cotswolds.
- **The Scottish Borders**: Trains from **Edinburgh** to **Galashiels** or **Melrose** take you to the tranquil landscapes of the Scottish Borders. This area offers beautiful walking trails, historic abbeys, and small towns that seem untouched by time.
- **Lake District**: From **Manchester** or **Oxenholme**, a short train ride will take you deep into the heart of the Lake District. Known for its hiking routes, tranquil lakes, and quaint villages, this region is a haven for outdoor enthusiasts.
- **Cornwall's Coastal Path**: The **Penzance** to **St Ives** route offers breathtaking views of Cornwall's rugged coastline. For the more adventurous, it's possible to walk sections of the **South West Coast Path** right from the station.

Traveling by train in 2026 offers an unparalleled opportunity to see Britain from a unique perspective. With comfortable accommodations, spectacular views, and easy access to some of the most iconic destinations, rail travel is both practical and enriching. By following these tips and planning your trip carefully, you can make the most of your journey, whether you're traveling for leisure, adventure, or simply to explore the beauty of the British landscape by rail.

BOOKING TICKETS & RAIL PASSES FOR BEST VALUE

Exploring Britain by train is one of the most scenic and convenient ways to travel, but understanding ticket options and rail passes is essential to getting the best value. From high-speed intercity routes to regional lines serving villages and natural landmarks, careful planning ensures both savings and flexibility. This guide explains how to book tickets, choose rail passes, and navigate the system efficiently, making your rail adventure smooth, economical, and enjoyable.

UNDERSTANDING THE UK RAIL NETWORK

Britain's rail network is extensive, connecting major cities, historic towns, and scenic regions. Trains are operated by multiple companies, including **Avanti West Coast, Great Western Railway, Northern Rail, ScotRail,** and **Transport for Wales**, with services often overlapping in key hubs.

- **Intercity routes:** Fast trains connecting major cities, such as London to Edinburgh, London to Bristol, or Manchester to Glasgow.
- **Regional services:** Slower trains linking smaller towns, countryside destinations, and scenic areas like the **Lake District**, **Snowdonia**, or **the Cotswolds**.
- **Rural & heritage lines:** Scenic lines such as the **West Highland Line** or **Ffestiniog Railway** often require separate tickets or rail pass add-ons.

Understanding whether you're traveling on a high-speed intercity train or a local branch line helps in selecting the right ticket or pass.

Ticket Types

Advance Tickets

- **Definition:** Pre-purchased tickets for a specific train at a fixed price, often cheaper than flexible fares.
- **Advantages:** Can save up to 60% compared to on-the-day prices, especially for long-distance travel.
- **Limitations:** Must be used on the train and time booked; changes or refunds are usually restricted.

Tip: Book early, particularly for popular routes such as **London to Edinburgh** or **London to the West Country**, to secure the lowest fares.

Off-Peak and Super Off-Peak

- **Off-Peak:** Valid outside busy commuting times; often mid-morning, midday, and late evening.
- **Super Off-Peak:** Even lower fares than standard Off-Peak, with more restricted times.

Practical Insight: Off-Peak tickets are ideal for sightseeing trips to places like **Bath, Conwy, or the Lake District**, allowing flexible travel without the stress of peak-hour trains.

Anytime Tickets

- **Definition:** Flexible tickets valid on any train, any time.
- **Advantages:** Ideal if your schedule may change, or if traveling on busy scenic lines during peak season.
- **Cost:** Typically, the most expensive ticket type; best for convenience or last-minute travel.

Railcards: Discounts for Frequent and Eligible Travelers

Railcards offer significant savings—usually 1/3 off most fares—and cater to different groups:

- **16–25 Railcard:** For young adults and students.
- **Senior Railcard:** Age 60+, offers discounts on both train fares and many attractions.
- **Two Together Railcard:** For two people traveling together, ideal for couples or friends.
- **Family & Friends Railcard:** Up to four adults and four children can save 1/3 off fares, excellent for family trips.

Practical Tip: Railcards often cover both standard and Off-Peak tickets, making them especially valuable for day trips or longer journeys in scenic regions.

RAIL PASSES FOR MULTI-REGION TRAVEL

For travelers planning extensive rail journeys, rail passes offer convenience and savings:

BritRail Pass

- **Coverage:** Unlimited travel on National Rail services throughout England, Scotland, and Wales.
- **Types:** Consecutive day passes or flexible days within a month.
- **Best For:** Visitors planning multiple long journeys, such as London to the Lake District, then onwards to Edinburgh, Snowdonia, or the West Highland Line.

Regional Passes

- **Scotland: Spirit of Scotland Travelpass** allows unlimited rail and bus travel throughout Scotland.
- **Wales: Explore Wales Pass** covers trains and buses connecting scenic areas like **Snowdonia**, the **Brecon Beacons**, and coastal towns.
- **England:** Regional passes exist for the **South West**, **Yorkshire**, and the **Lake District**, ideal for exploring a concentrated area without buying multiple tickets.

Personal Insight: Passes are cost-effective if planning two or more long rail journeys or visiting multiple destinations over several days. For example, a BritRail pass for a week can cover London–Edinburgh, a Lake District loop, and a West Highland adventure, saving both money and hassle compared to individual tickets.

Booking Platforms and Tools

Online Booking

- **National Rail Enquiries:** Comprehensive platform for timetables, fares, and station information.
- **Train Operators:** Direct websites such as **Avanti West Coast**, **Great Western Railway**, and **ScotRail** often have the best Advance fares.
- **Third-Party Sites: Trainline** or **Rail Europe** are user-friendly for international visitors but may include small booking fees.

Tip: Compare Advance and Off-Peak fares across multiple platforms to find the best deal.

Ticket Collection and E-Tickets

- Many tickets are **print-at-home** or **mobile**.
- Station ticket machines or counters allow **collection of pre-booked tickets**.
- Some scenic or rural lines may require **paper tickets**, so check before departure.

Timing and Planning

- **Peak vs Off-Peak Travel:** Peak hours (roughly 6:30–9:30 and 16:30–19:00 on weekdays) are more expensive and crowded.

- **Weekend Travel:** Often quieter on intercity trains; Off-Peak tickets may start earlier, increasing flexibility.
- **Seasonal Tips:** Summer and school holidays attract tourists to scenic lines, so book Advance tickets for routes like **West Highland Line** or **Conwy Valley Line** well in advance.

Combining Rail Travel with Local Transport

- Many scenic or rural destinations require connecting buses, shuttles, or ferries.
- Examples: From **Windermere station** to Ambleside (bus or lakeside walk), or from **Mallaig station** to ferry services for Skye or Eigg.
- Check train-bus connections when booking; some passes cover both rail and local buses.

Practical Insight: Planning transfers ahead saves time and ensures a seamless experience, especially in remote or mountainous areas.

Personal Tips for Maximizing Value

- Always **compare Advance and Off-Peak fares**. On scenic routes, Off-Peak may be more flexible with minimal cost difference.
- **Buy railcards** if eligible—they often pay for themselves in one or two journeys.
- **Use passes** strategically for multi-day tours across regions, combining rail with foot exploration.
- **Check station facilities:** Some small scenic stops have limited ticket machines, so buying ahead prevents delays.
- **Travel early for the best views** on scenic lines; window seats often provide the most memorable experience.

Personal Experience: On the West Highland Line, booking an Advance ticket months ahead saved over 50% compared to buying on the day. Paired with a BritRail Scotland pass, it allowed unlimited scenic journeys along the line and included rural branches without worrying about individual tickets.

Booking tickets and rail passes strategically can transform a UK rail trip from costly and stressful into flexible, scenic, and economical. Whether traveling between cities, exploring historic towns, or venturing into the Highlands, understanding ticket types, railcards, and regional passes ensures you get maximum value. Early planning, combining rail with local transport, and taking advantage of Off-Peak and Advance fares allows you to enjoy Britain's iconic and hidden landscapes without breaking the bank.

Rail travel is not just about getting from A to B; with the right tickets and passes, it becomes part of the adventure—connecting you effortlessly to historic sites, scenic vistas, and cultural gems across the UK.

NAVIGATING TRAIN STATIONS & TRANSFERS

Traveling Britain by train is one of the most scenic and convenient ways to explore the country, but for many, navigating stations and transfers can feel daunting. This guide focuses on practical advice, regional insights, and strategies to make every connection seamless, efficient, and even enjoyable.

UNDERSTANDING BRITISH TRAIN STATIONS

British train stations vary widely—from small rural stops to major city hubs. Knowing what to expect helps reduce stress and plan your journey effectively.

- **Major Stations:** London Paddington, Edinburgh Waverley, Glasgow Central, Birmingham New Street, and Manchester Piccadilly are large interchanges with multiple platforms, extensive signage, cafés, waiting areas, and luggage facilities.
- **Medium Stations:** Cities like York, Bristol Temple Meads, Exeter St Davids, and Oxford have fewer platforms but still offer ticket offices, small shops, and staffed help desks.
- **Rural & Minor Stations:** Stations such as Looe, St Ives, or Pitlochry are often unstaffed or partially staffed, with a single platform, timetable boards, and sometimes a ticket machine.

Traveler Tip: At smaller stations, always check train times in advance using National Rail or Transport for Wales apps, as frequency may be limited, especially on weekends or holidays.

Station Layout & Wayfinding

Stations are generally divided into key zones for easy navigation:

- **Ticketing & Information:** Ticket offices, machines, and information desks are usually near station entrances. Apps and online bookings are widely used, but it's wise to keep a printed or digital timetable for backup.

- **Platforms & Signage:** Platforms are numbered and clearly signed, with digital boards showing live train departures, destinations, and platform changes. Large stations often have footbridges, escalators, or lifts connecting platforms.

- **Waiting Areas & Amenities:** Seating, cafés, restrooms, and luggage storage are standard in larger stations. Some rural stations may only have a bench and shelter.

- **Accessibility:** Most major stations provide step-free access, tactile paving, and assistance services. Request help in advance for boarding if you have mobility needs.

Personal Insight: In my experience, arriving at least 15–20 minutes early at major hubs allows time to locate the correct platform, grab refreshments, and absorb live announcements for potential changes.

PLANNING TRANSFERS BETWEEN TRAINS

Transfers can involve the same station or multiple stations in a city. Planning and understanding connections is key:

- **Single-Station Transfers:** Many journeys require only a platform change within the same station. Check departure boards for platform numbers, as they can change quickly.

- **Multi-Station Transfers:** In cities like London or Glasgow, you may need to transfer between stations—e.g., London Paddington to London King's Cross. Allow extra time for taxis, Underground, or buses.

- **Regional Transfers:** In rural areas, transfers may involve buses or taxis from the nearest station to your destination. For example, reaching the Brecon Beacons or Cornwall's coastal villages often requires a short bus or taxi ride from a mainline station.

Traveler Tip: Build at least 20–30 minutes between connecting trains at major hubs, and at least 45–60 minutes if you must switch stations in a city.

Using Station Facilities Efficiently

British stations offer amenities that can simplify travel and make waiting comfortable:

- **Ticket Machines & Collection Points:** Use machines for last-minute purchases or to collect pre-booked tickets. Larger stations have multiple machines, reducing queues.

- **Cafés & Quick Meals:** Most major stations have cafés or fast-food options. In rural stations, bring your own snacks if services are limited.

- **Luggage Storage:** Left luggage lockers are available at larger stations, useful if you want to explore nearby towns before catching a connecting train.

- **Restrooms & Waiting Areas:** Keep in mind that smaller stations may have limited facilities or be closed outside staffed hours.

Personal Insight: At stations like Edinburgh Waverley or London Paddington, a coffee in the waiting area overlooking the cityscape adds a relaxed start to your journey.

Timetables, Apps, and Real-Time Information

Staying informed is crucial for smooth transfers:

- **National Rail App & Websites:** Check live departure boards, platform numbers, and delays. Set alerts for your train to avoid missing connections.

- **Transport-Specific Apps:** ScotRail, GWR, and other regional apps provide updates, seat reservations, and local transfer information.

- **Printed Timetables:** Still valuable at rural stations where mobile reception may be limited.

Travel Insight: During disruptions, staff are the fastest source of information—don't hesitate to ask at ticket offices or information points.

Connecting to Local Transport

Often, your train journey is only part of your trip. Understanding local transport helps access destinations efficiently:

- **Buses & Coaches:** Major stations are usually bus hubs. Check local schedules, especially in rural areas where services may be infrequent.

- **Taxis & Rideshares:** Taxis are generally available at all major stations; smaller stations may require pre-booking.

- **Walking & Cycling:** Some destinations, like St Ives or Oxford city center, are easily reached on foot from the station. Many stations provide secure bicycle storage for onward exploration.

Personal Insight: Combining rail with a short local bus ride often reveals hidden corners of Britain that are inaccessible by car, especially in coastal or rural areas.

Seasonal and Regional Considerations

Station facilities, train frequency, and transfer times vary depending on location and season:

- **Summer:** Tourist destinations like Cornwall, the Lake District, and Scottish Highlands are busy. Book trains early, and allow extra time at stations for crowds.
- **Winter:** Shorter daylight hours and occasional delays from snow or ice require earlier departures and flexible connections.
- **Rural Routes:** Stations in rural Wales, Yorkshire, and the Highlands may operate infrequent services—double-check schedules to avoid long waits.

Travel Tip: Always have a contingency plan for missed connections, including alternative train times, buses, or taxis.

Tips for Stress-Free Transfers

- Travel light when possible; luggage can slow down transfers.
- Familiarize yourself with station maps in advance, available on National Rail or station websites.
- Allow extra time for ticket collection, restrooms, and finding platforms.
- Keep essential items like train tickets, ID, and a mobile device in an easily accessible pocket.
- For multi-leg journeys, consider advance reservations for both trains and connecting local transport.

Personal Insight: I always carry a compact guidebook or map of the local area—especially helpful when transferring to bus services for remote destinations like the Brecon Beacons or North Cornwall.

Practical Transfer Map Example

- **London Paddington → St Ives:** Direct train to St Erth, change for St Ives Bay Line. Station walks to town center or café.
- **Edinburgh Waverley → Inverness:** Direct ScotRail service. Optional stops at Perth or Pitlochry for short walks.
- **Cardiff Central → Brecon Beacons:** Train to Merthyr Tydfil, then bus/taxi to Brecon or nearby villages.

This shows the importance of planning each leg, combining rail, bus, taxi, and walking for efficient exploration.

Navigating Britain's train stations and transfers is straightforward with preparation, awareness, and a few practical strategies. Understanding station layouts, timetables, and local transport connections allows travelers to move confidently from city centers to rural or coastal destinations. Combining trains with walking or short bus rides opens access to hidden gems and scenic landscapes that are often missed by car. By planning ahead and remaining flexible, every transfer becomes part of the adventure rather than a source of stress.

SEASONAL INSIGHTS: BEST TIME TO TRAVEL FOR SCENIC JOURNEYS

Britain's landscapes transform dramatically with the seasons. From the snow-dusted Scottish Highlands to the golden autumn hedgerows of Devon, timing your train journey can profoundly enhance your experience. This guide provides practical seasonal insights for scenic rail travel, including regional highlights, weather considerations, cultural events, and tips for making the most of each season.

SPRING: FRESH LANDSCAPES AND BLOOMING VIEWS

Timing and Weather

- March to May marks spring in Britain, with mild temperatures and lengthening daylight.
- Weather is variable: sunny spells are interspersed with light showers. Layered clothing and waterproof jackets are recommended.

Scenic Highlights

- **Lake District:** Snow-capped peaks gradually give way to vibrant green valleys and blooming wildflowers. Early spring is ideal for photography as the fells remain uncrowded.

- **Scottish Highlands:** Rivers swell with melting snow; rhododendrons and wildflowers emerge in glens.

- **South Coast and Devon:** Coastal cliffs and hedgerows display fresh greenery. Gower Peninsula and Cornwall's beaches bloom with spring flowers.

Travel Tips

- Rail travel is generally quiet outside school holidays, providing unobstructed window views.

- Morning light enhances landscapes; consider early departures to capture sunrise over lochs or estuaries.

- National Trust properties and castles often open by late March, offering access before summer crowds.

Cultural and Culinary Insight

- Spring menus feature local lamb, asparagus, and early seafood.

- Festivals: Edinburgh International Science Festival, RHS Chelsea Flower Show (accessible via train from London), and regional agricultural shows highlight local culture.

SUMMER: LONG DAYS AND VIBRANT COASTLINES

Timing and Weather

- June to August brings long daylight hours, warmer temperatures, and relatively stable weather, though coastal and highland areas can still be windy.

- Peak tourist season means trains, accommodations, and attractions are busy—advance booking is essential.

Scenic Highlights

- **Coastal Routes:** Devon, Cornwall, Pembrokeshire, and Northumberland coastlines are at their most vivid. Waves, cliffs, and sandy beaches are bathed in sunlight.
- **Countryside:** Cotswolds, Peak District, and Yorkshire Dales feature lush green fields, meadows in bloom, and full river levels.
- **Scottish Highlands and Islands:** Long daylight allows exploration of remote islands like Skye, Orkney, and Shetland, with dramatic landscapes at dawn and dusk.

Travel Tips

- Choose window seats on the left-hand side heading west for optimal coastal views in Devon and Cornwall.
- Pack sun protection and light layers; some trains may lack air conditioning.
- Early morning trains help avoid crowds at popular stops like St Ives, Tenby, or Fort William.

Cultural and Culinary Insight

- Summer food markets showcase fresh seafood, berries, and artisan produce.
- Coastal towns host festivals: St Ives September Festival (arts), Tenby Fish Week, and Highland Games events.
- Outdoor dining is ideal; harbor-side pubs and cliff-top cafés offer local ales, cider, and seafood.

AUTUMN: GOLDEN HUES AND QUIET VILLAGES

Timing and Weather

- September to November brings cooler temperatures, crisp air, and gradually shorter days.
- Rain increases in late autumn, particularly in western coastal regions. Pack waterproofs and layered clothing.

Scenic Highlights

- **Woodlands and Valleys:** Peak autumn foliage in the Lake District, Yorkshire Dales, and Cotswolds offers vivid golds, reds, and browns.

- **Coastlines:** Golden light enhances cliff and beach scenery; stormy skies create dramatic photography opportunities along Devon, Cornwall, and Pembrokeshire.
- **Highlands:** Autumn mists add atmosphere to glens, lochs, and castles. Wildlife spotting improves as deer, birds, and marine animals are more active near shorelines.

Travel Tips

- Trains and accommodations are quieter than summer, offering a more relaxed pace.
- Evening light is excellent for coastal photography, while mid-morning sun enhances inland valleys.
- Short hikes along the South West Coast Path or Northumberland cliffs are particularly rewarding in autumn color.

Cultural and Culinary Insight

- Seasonal menus feature game, root vegetables, and freshly caught seafood.
- Harvest festivals, agricultural shows, and food fairs offer opportunities to sample local produce.
- Village pubs provide cozy refuge after walks; try mulled cider or warming seafood chowders.

WINTER: SNOW, STORMS, AND ATMOSPHERIC LANDSCAPES

Timing and Weather

- December to February features short days, cold temperatures, and occasional snow inland and in the Highlands. Coastal areas are milder but can be stormy.
- Dress in warm layers, waterproofs, and sturdy footwear for walking and photography.

Scenic Highlights

- **Scottish Highlands:** Snow-dusted peaks and frozen lochs create iconic winter imagery.
- **Coastal Regions:** Winter storms along Devon, Cornwall, and Pembrokeshire reveal the raw power of the sea.

- **Countryside:** Misty mornings, frosted fields, and quiet villages offer a sense of solitude and stillness.

Travel Tips

- Off-peak trains provide quieter journeys and more flexibility.
- Daylight is limited; plan short scenic walks near stations or accessible viewpoints.
- Storm-watching and dramatic coastal photography are winter highlights; check tide tables and weather advisories.

Cultural and Culinary Insight

- Winter menus highlight hearty stews, roasted meats, and warming puddings.
- Seasonal markets, Christmas fairs, and New Year events provide local flavor and cultural immersion.
- Snow or frost can transform historic towns and castles into photographic highlights.

Regional Highlights by Season

- **Scotland:** Autumn for foliage in Cairngorms, winter for Highland's snow, summer for island exploration.
- **South West England:** Summer for beaches and coastal walks, spring for wildflowers and mild hiking, autumn for golden hedgerows.
- **Wales:** Spring for valleys and rivers, summer for Pembrokeshire coast, winter for quiet Snowdonia exploration.
- **Northern England:** Autumn for Dales and Moors, summer for Lake District lakes, winter for atmospheric village photography.

PRACTICAL TRAVEL ADVICE FOR SEASONAL PLANNING

- **Layering:** Prepare for changing weather; pack waterproofs, gloves, and hats in autumn and winter, and light layers in spring and summer.
- **Advance Bookings:** Summer and holiday periods require early tickets; spring and autumn are ideal for flexible travel.
- **Accommodation:** Coastal villages fill quickly in peak season; inland inns and countryside B&Bs offer quieter alternatives.

- **Photography:** Light quality changes with season; winter and autumn provide dramatic skies, summer offers golden long days, and spring gives soft, fresh lighting.
- **Local Insight:** Check seasonal closures for attractions, heritage sites, and ferry services, especially in winter and early spring.

Slow Travel Experience Across Seasons

Seasonal travel transforms the scenic railway experience. Slow travel—taking trains, walking short sections, and pausing in villages—allows full immersion in each season's unique character.

- Spring offers freshness and solitude before the tourist rush.
- Summer emphasizes color, long walks, and coastal vibrancy.
- Autumn highlights golden landscapes, seasonal cuisine, and quiet charm.
- Winter emphasizes dramatic weather, reflective photography, and intimate village experiences.

Layering train travel with short hikes, local buses, and exploration of towns ensures travelers enjoy the seasonal contrasts of Britain fully.

Timing your scenic train journeys in Britain can enhance every aspect of travel: landscapes, wildlife, food, and cultural experiences. Spring brings bloom and mild light, summer offers long days and vibrant coasts, autumn showcases golden foliage and quieter villages, and winter delivers atmospheric vistas and dramatic weather. Consider regional highlights, seasonal cuisine, and practical transport logistics when planning, and embrace slow travel to connect deeply with Britain's landscapes throughout the year.

Manufactured by Amazon.ca
Bolton, ON